Success is Not by Chance

AshokIndu

DIAMOND BOOKS
www.diamondbooks.in

Publisher	**:**	**Diamond Pocket Books (P) Ltd.** X-30, Okhla Industrial Area, Phase-II New Delhi-110020
Phone	:	011-40712200
E-mail	:	wecare@diamondbooks.in
Website	:	www.diamondbooks.in
Edition	:	2025

Success is not by Chance
by: *AshokIndu*

Dedicated to my parents
Late Sri S N Pandey
and Smt. R Pandey

The surest way to make a task more difficult is to put it off to a later date.

–Ralph Marston

Foreword

Success is Not by Chance is my third book. Our youngsters are the future of our country. I have written this book keeping them in mind. They are brimming with energy and new ideas all the time. If they channelize their energies in a positive direction, they can achieve unknown heights in their life and career. This book is an effort to channelize the energies of the youth towards a constructive direction.

The middle-aged people, veterans, office goers and even housewives would enjoy reading this book. That is because everyone wants to succeed in his or her work. I have used simple principles and supporting examples to help all readers grab the gist of the success process.

One does not need magical powers to succeed. You always have a perfect brain and the will to succeed. Hence, the basic ingredients of success are within yourself! That is what I have tried to convey in this book.

People fear the unknown. They fear that their business would incur loss. They think that their plans would go haywire. The more they fear, the more this fear overpowers them. Why do they have fear? Believe in yourself and your abilities. Remove all fears first. Then, go ahead and grab all opportunities that come to you. That way, success would come to your life.

Keep polishing your skills in every phase of your life.Never give up. Make plans and execute them. Success requires only moderate intelligence but devoted action. Do your tasks with passion and complete dedication. That is the right procedure for attaining fortune and fame in any field. Devoted concentration, not big, boisterous thinkers, brings success.

I thank my wife, Indu Pandey, who worked as hard as I to complete this wonderful book. Probably, her contribution is much more than mine. Further, I thank the publishers (Diamond Books) and their DTP staff who brought this book into fine shape. Finally, I thank all those people, my friends and guides, who gave useful suggestions from time to time to prepare the fine content for this book.

The author, publisher, and DTP team have left no stone unturned to produce a good book for our valued readers. However, some mistakes may have crept in due to human or machine errors. Our valued readers are requested to point them out so that the next edition of this book may be a better presentation.

–AshokIndu

Dated: Oct. 17, 2009

Pandey Education Trust
(A Trusted Name in Quality Education Consultancy Services)
2, Puran Badi, Model Town C, Malviya Nagar,
Jaipur-302017, Rajasthan (India)

To the Readers

We do believe that you are born to win. However, as soon as you start working on a task or project, you feel that completing it is not so easy and that you may or may not complete it. When we become day-dreamers, we get many negative feelings (or thoughts). It is a natural process. I want you to do day-dreaming but at the same time, think of winning. This book is precisely about this very concept. If you channelize your thoughts in a positive direction (I must win ... I must win), then you will succeed!

Our brain works in the direction in which we initiate our thought process. Once you start thinking in a particular direction, you would be amazed to notice that you would not be able to divert your attention from that thought or ambition. As you increase the focus, you would be more determined to complete that act or achieve that goal. A determined individual can do miracles.

All successful people had some determination, an instinct, that they would achieve a particular goal. They achieved their respective goals in the long run!

The total solar eclipse took place on 22nd July, 2009. The NASA generated a 200-page report about this event. That was because it would not happen again before 2013 AD. NASA had stated that the best place to 'see' the eclipse was Taregana, a small place in Bihar. Aryabhatta, the famous Indian astrologer and mathematician, had studied planetary movements at this very place fifteen hundred years ago. He had worked here during the reign of the Mauryas. He had chosen this place to carry out his experiments, after wandering here and there in search of a good site.

Is that a mere coincidence? For many phenomena and events, proper scientific explanation could not be given till date. The only fact that has been proved is that human beings are the best and most intelligent animals on this earth. They can control nature and even destroy it by using their knowledge. You are a human being. You can also mould the situations as per your thinking. The only pre-condition is – have the determination to mould the situation. Without the magic called determination, you cannot change the situation.

No doubt, you are born to win! That is because you are determined to achieve something. In order to do a miracle or perform better than others, you do not need more than two hands and one head. Further, always ask the Almighty for the boon of determination, nothing else. These two hands, one head and determination would help you get whatever you would demand from life!

We always have doubts about our capabilities. We try to take suggestions from others. We never try to evaluate ourselves. Thus, the consequences are harmful, even fatal. Has anyone with high IQ and intelligence achieved something extraordinary? Most inventors and discoverers, who got themselves named in the Forbes List, were ordinary people! They were less intelligent than their friends! They had quit school or college. But all of them had just one trait as common – determination! They were determined to do or achieve something. Success does not require specific qualities but it only needs the refinement of qualities you already possess. Anything in this world is not a chance event but is the result of tireless, determined efforts. Only weak people use the phrase "by chance or due to luck." Such people do not believe in hard labour; they lack determination too.

Determine and be sure that nothing which you can dream is beyond your reach. You have all the ingredients to become a successful individual. You can become successful if you have the firm determination to succeed.

One thing is pretty sure – you have already started moving in a direction that would lead you to success. This is quite evident from the fact that you have chosen this book to read!

Be determined – and success shall be yours!

AshokIndu

Contents

Chapter I: Fuel Your Passion 13
- lKnow Your Worth 16
- Develop Inbuilt Qualities 18
- Decide Your Destiny 20
- Sharpen Your Skills 23
- Be firm with Your Thinking 26
- Believe in Fate but Keep Trying 27
- Prove Your Individuality 30
- Believe in Yourself 31
- Follow Momentum Equation 33
- Remove Fear of Failure 35

Chapter II: Preserve Your Positive Energy 38
- Preserve Positive Energy 40
- Be Confident 42
- Always be Happy 43
- Dare to be Successful 46
- Learn from Other's Mistakes 48
- Determined to Get the Result 51
- Take Timely Action 54
- Empower Yourself 55
- Be Firm in Action 60
- All Professions are Rewarding 64

Chapter III: Get Motivated Everyday 68
- Go For Day Dreaming 71
- Change Your Attitude 74

- Don't Care for Everyone 78
- Avoid Criticising 80
- Everything and Everyone is not Bad 83
- Always Be Positive 84
- Satisfy yourself with What You have 86
- Success is a Continuous Process 88
- Success is not Sudden 90
- Every Problem has a Solution 92

Chapter – IV: Create Your Own World 95
- Have Faith in Yourself 98
- Contentment and Saving for Future 100
- Do What You Feel is Right 103
- Never Shake anyone's Faith 106
- Master Your Attitude 108
- Don't be Afraid of Criticism 111
- Be Part of the Solution 114
- Review Progress Daily 116
- Treat Past as History 119
- Be Committed Towards Your Action 122

Chapter – V: Attitude– The Deciding Factor of Success 125
- Make the Thing to Happen 128
- Failure is Natural 132
- Mistakes Are a Boon 135
- Feel Comfortable Wherever You Are 139
- Always Have the Wish to Win 141
- You Can Do It 144
- Unlock Your Potential 147
- Be Firm 148

Chapter 1

Fuel Your Passion

An eight-year-old boy approached an old man, looked into his eyes and asked, "I understand you're a very wise man. I'd like to know the secret of life." The old man looked down at the youngster and replied, I've thought a lot in my lifetime and the secret can be summed up in four words. Here are these:

1. Think: This means think about the values you wish to live your life by.
2. Believe: This means believe in yourself based on the thinking you've framed about the values you're going to have in your life.

3. Dream: This means dream about the things that can be, based on your values and beliefs.
4. Dare: This means dare to make your dreams become reality; you would be required to combine think; believe, and 'dream' to dare.

And with that, Walt E. Disney said to little boy, "Think, Believe, Dream and Dare."

The visualization of anything is the result of the thinking we have in our mind. This thinking is the result of our beliefs. If we believe that we can, we start thinking in that direction only. Your thinking can get a concrete shape once you have a firm belief that something can happen. If we feel that consulting a doctor is not going to give us any relief, be sure, irrespective of the best treatment by the doctor, we will not be able to give any relief. It is mere belief which makes most of the things happen in this world. Sometimes, we feel that we have achieved what we desired due to our hard labour and destiny whereas the fact is that we achieved something in our life since we had started believing in our thinking dreamed something based on our belief and dared to act in the direction of that dream fulfillment. This is what a balanced and exemplary life is!

It has been scientifically proved that one gets a reaction for one's actions in our daily life. We visualize something. We swung to action to achieve our visualization, with a firm belief that we have the stamina to achieve the same and we really achieve what we intend to achieve.

Life is like a flute. It has many holes and is hollow but if we use air blow through our lips, it produces magical music.

We are born free and so is our thinking. We may or may not have control over our thinking. The factor which plays crucial role in changing our thinking into actions is our will power. It navigates us towards our goal with firm belief and action. Our action is the by-product of our thinking as it follows the famous law of nature propounded by Newton. He had said, "To every action, there is an equal and opposite reaction." Your actions are shaped according to the ideas simmering inside you.

Most of us feel that we are in a position to do and comment in the way we like. We are living in an independent country which gives us the right to criticize even the top brass of the country. Not only that, we are free to take out our shoe and throw it at the head of the strongest person on this earth in front of the whole world, as if we were the only person who have got the guts to revolt against the system.

We fail to understand here that everyone and everything will not go according to our wishes in this world. We must know our limitations and appreciate and respect the independence of others. We are dependent upon the thinking of the people around us as we can never operate in isolation.

Remember the famous experiment of Archimedes in which he had put a coin and a feather in vacuum glass. He turned the glass upside down both the coin and feather touched the surface at the same time. But you will not be able to execute this experiment in a normal atmosphere where the coin will touch the earth surface much faster than the feather due to its weight. This experiment is true for individuals like us too. The astronauts going to the moon can jump like monkeys on the lunar surface as there is no atmosphere; the same is not possible on the earth where there is gravitational force on every individual.

We are born independent but just after taking birth, we become part of the bigger ecosystem which controls this earth and any slight variation in the system will bring the system in crisis. We have to fuel our passion but by taking care of the system, lest we should become extinct in due course of time. It is important for our survival and we understand it clearly that our passion is an individualistic approach whereas continuation of the system is our compulsion. We can be here if the system persists and without it, our own identity has no meaning.

Know your worth

Ghajini, a movie churned out by Bollywood, was a blockbuster release of 2008. Mr. Perfectionist, Amir Khan, received appreciation from all due to it. This movie did soaring business which none of other films did, so say cinema critics. I am not a lover of films but I appreciate the role of Hindi films in uniting our diverse India. My kids forced me to watch the movie and I agreed on a condition that I will see it on my lap top as I could control the movement of the film that way.

It was the last week of 2008 and I was forced to leave from the office a bit early to watch this movie. After I finished, it I was surprised, why Indian movies had become the case history for management students. The film was so exciting that one couldn't get bored at any point of time. I can't forget the best two lines of the film which made the difference between pride and commitment. I can write a motivational book for the young generation is my commitment, but I can only write a motivational book for young generation will reflect my pride..

The hero of the movie overpowers his fears by making a constant endeavour for the same. He did it as he wanted to do that and not because he was forced to do something. He utilises his positive energy to overpower his fears and is successful but sometimes, some persons may try to overpower their fears by utilizing some negative forces and thus, make the situation further worst.

Some people must have witnessed the famous writer Vikram Seth opening a wine bottle on the stage in a literary concert for school students; the concert was organised at Jaipur. I am not against the consumption of wine by anyone as I don't take but I am against any such flatulence which, not add any thing positive to one's image. Everyone born on this earth has some strengths and weakness. However, why should one reflect such weakness publicly without a positive gain? It is nothing else than the fear of failure at a point of time.

We all are sometimes wrapped with some foolish pride and try to cover ourselves with such prejudices as spoil our positive traits. It happens because we are not sure of our capabilities and have a strong fear of failure. In order to avoid the same, most of the times, we keep ourselves wrapped in a shell. Only a thought of making ourself ready to face the situation makes all the difference and we must learn this tact to lead a happy and fearless life. No one will be able to fine tune oneself all of a sudden. However, with regular practice and change of mind set, it is possible. We have to remember that no one in this world will be able to achieve anything irrespective of his worth and competence without having a control on his fears. They are the main enemy of success which you have to combat first before starting your journey towards success.

Most failures in life are the true victims of fear.

Develop inbuilt qualities

Even an individual having superb qualities gets defeated in the race for achieving something whereas another having less capabilities and doing far less labour gets what he desires. It is not luck at all but it is only his perseverance which makes him winner in the race of success. This lack of perservance makes the other person a loser. Most of us, who are unsuccessful in our endeavours, are so due to the lack of perseverance and no other factor is directly responsible for this phenomenon. Perseverance is the will of chasing something without taking any rest. The hare was sure to defeat the tortoise in the race but it was lack perseverance on his part led him defeat in the race. That had he tortoise had nothing to loose and, above all, he was more consistent then the here.

Perseverance is the will of chasing something without taking any chance.

In this race, the only thing which was certain was the defeat of tortoise. It was preordained but he overturned his destiny and won the race only due to his sheer perseverance. On the other hand, the hare lost due to his overconfidence and pride.

The tortoise, being sure of his defeat, won as he chased the goal without taking rest. It happens with most of us that after achieving something, we become sure of our competence; and our downfall starts from there. We must have the perseverance of the tortoise when we want to change our destiny and force it to favour us.

One can't do justice to oneself without having this killer instinct within him. Perseverance is a learnable quality. Being a learnable quality, it can be acquired by feeling the need for the same. The feeling of being a gainer or a looser starts first within ourself in the same way in which the head of the fish starts deteriorating first after its death. No one can avoid this thinking but there are a few who overpower this thinking with another thinking that let me see what can happen?

Success is like a "quality trait" found in a hunter. A hunter goes on chasing his prey till he gets a chance to overpower it. In this race, he gets defeated many a times but still he never stops trying. At last, he gets his prey. He learns the chasing quality from his parents and knows that running behind the prey is his destiny. This very learnable quality of chasing the goal is the elementary principle of success.

A person who is trying to excel in the area of his choice must go on till he gets what he desired at the outset without compromising with the goal. Most of us learn the quality of compromising than that of chasing. We do so as it is easy to compromise and feel relaxed than go on for the chasing quality. Psychologically, it is easier to get satisfied with whatever we get than strive up to the last moment for what exactly we want.

Success is not the domain of intelligent persons. Research has proved that anyone, who has the quality of chasing his goal, achieves, it irrespective of the intelligence quotient he possesses. Intelligence is only one of the basic prerequisites for achieving success. A person having high IQ and striving for success will have an edge over a person having lower IQ. However, tragedy is that the people possessing high IQ values are so much engrossed in their work that they generally lack perseverance, the main quality to achieve success. From the very beginning, the persons having high IQ values think that they are the best and can achieve anything they desire. That time never comes in their life and they fail in the end.

Success requires the combination of characteristics and most of these characteristics are learnable. Anyone can be born rich but no one can be born successful. In order to be successful, one has to strive for success. One has to decide one's destiny to be successful, else one has to decide to remain a fiasco. Once you decide your destiny, you go on getting the required qualities that would push you in the direction of your goal.

Decide your destiny

Once you are ready to face the challenges of life, be sure that no one will be able to deviate you from your "follow the success route" instinct. Your perseverance is your quality and you can never be out of that once you decide to see the end of the task started by you. We know that a happening or an act is not permanent but still, we are unable to control our feelings. I remember the day when after having topped the entrance test of the top engineering college of India, my son refused to study there after the first year. It was very difficult for me to come out of that shock.

I was disturbed till I reached my son's hostel after an overnight journey by train. I saw the gloomy face of my son and immediately asked him will he think again to continue his study there being the top engineering college of India. At that times he was not a boy of eighteen but was looking like a four-year kid having the same innocent face when I had carried him in my lap. He did not answer my question but kept his head down and that was my answer.

Sometimes, you have to observe someone and get the answer without asking for an answer. I told my son to pack up his entire baggage. We boarded the evening train bound for our home town the next morning. I told my wife to be normal. I admit that she has more potency of early recovery than I had. We both took it nonchalantly and he was admitted to an engineering college of our city. I can't predict his future but immediately after finishing his studies he got a nice placement in the cement industry. We did not recall that episode and never cared for the loss of money. But the dividend we are getting now is far more than the money which was wasted.

For every person on this earth, all situations arise but the handling of such situations differs with persons, places and time. If that is so, it is an acceptable term but if the reaction of an individual does not change with the person, place and time, one should be careful with such people. The reason is that people like these will be having very strong liking and disliking and this is not correct in this age of globalization. The worth of an individual is measured during adverse circumstances only. What we are and what we are not depends upon the situation which we are handling.

There was a tradition in a management institute that ten of its top students used to get selected by one of the top groups of the State after finishing their examinations. It had been going on for years. In the recent past, the topper among the top ten was rejected by the company on the plea that he was not fluent in English.

It was the time when MNCs had started penetrating the Indian Job Markets. The boy was disturbed; he as well as all others used to condemn his luck. Just after six months, the boy was called by a company whose specific need was a topper of the premier management school but not so fluent in English. The firm wanted to launch the product for ordinary Indians an ordinary Indian. The boy got that job; it carried status and salary much higher than those of his colleagues.

Be sure that chance sometimes may not click but when it clicks, you will not be able to hold it if you do not have the means to use it.

You will always get people around you who will tell you that they take everything by heart. There is nothing wrong in this action but the problem is with the after-effect. Taking something to our heart and making ourselves burdened with a situation may not give us anything except repentance. Situations may force us to take some unpleasant decisions but our worth will be measured during adverse circumstances only. In case we have got control over our feelings, we have a chance to recover; and it will bring respect for us from all persons around us.

> **Situations may force you to take some unpleasant, harsh decisions but your worth would be measured during adverse circumstances only.**

You might have heard that a young lady had lost her husband in an accident or a mother had lost her only son who had just completed his administrative service training and so on. If these suffering people could muster the strength to recover from the loss, it would have been much better? I am not advising to you follow The Gita and start behaving like a saint but only telling you that you must act like a person who should be different from others. It is our thinking which makes us different from others, for our thinking is reflected by our actions.

Sharpen your skills

People generally feel that it is the university degree that makes someone successful. No doubt, that it is the basic requirement in life but it is basic only. There is no relations between being successful in life and a university degree. You must have noticed that people having high IQ values often work for people having the lowest IQ values. IIT and graduates from the premier management institutes are respected in world for their knowledge and skills. However, the top line of command that recruited them had never been to these institutions.

A huge boulder was lying on the main road, creating problems for passers-by as well as the moving vehicles. People complained to the municipal office. Thus, a group of engineers came to the site with labourers. The discussion went on. Someone was suggesting that the boulder should be blasted with a detonator and the debris should be thrown somewhere else. The total cost of the process would be around twenty thousand rupees. Another suggestion was to move it to one side but it was not feasible, for the boulder was huge. The conversation was going on and the labourers were waiting for instructions to start their work. In the mean time an old labourer from the lot stood up and told the chief engineer that in a day, they would be able to dig the earth and make a pit of the size of the boulder. Then, they would roll the piece into the dug pit and make the road plain with the help of the dug soil. The chief engineer looked at the labourer waited for a while and ordered the procedure to be done.

We require a basic degree to get ourselves established in a job but success in job will depend upon utilization of common sense. There is no course for developing common sense in any Indian or foreign university, except a new course started by an NGO in Ranchi (Bihar) to teach people to become politicians. I think Bihar (including Jharkhand) only deserves such courses and no other state in India can think of such an innovative course to drain the hard-earned money and energy. I am a Bihari too and have seen Biharis who aspire either to be IAS officers or politicians.

We have to sharpen our skills of decision making on the basis of our common sense. The earned degrees and diplomas can only be of some essential requirements for a profession. However, every job whether it is technical or non technical, requires basic skills that are the direct result of our observations.

You must have noticed that at entry level, there are always thousands of applications. As you go higher, the number of applications go on reducing because jobs go on being specific and you require basic skills to carry out such jobs. Formal education helps in minimizing your learning time. An educated person takes less time in understanding a difficult situation than a less educated person. However one cannot say that the uneducated person will never understand the situation. It is the time factor which differentiates an uneducated from educated. An educated person grasps the instructions in much lesser time. I don't know whether you know that even today, the main accountants of established business houses of India are still the descendents of the earliest (illiterate) accountant who had served them during those days. These business houses have a force of experienced chartered accounts and financial advisors with the best softwares to satisfy the government regulations but the backbone of their business is the old guards who never had a professional degree or diploma. They had inherited these skills from old generations.

Education brings you near the stairs leading to success but you yourself have to climb those stairs to taste the fruits of success.

A class of forty students receives the same education and all wish to get the same achievement. However, it does not happen and will never happens, every one will get equal reward. You may think that it is due to individual differences. However, nature has given everyone a brain of the same weight, in all adults, its weight is nearly 1400 grams. Education paves the way to understanding. An educated person understands the situation and takes precautionary measures more easily than an uneducated one. That is the only advantage an educated person has over an uneducated one, in the rest of the areas, responses of both person will be almost similar.

Be firm with your thinking

Nowadays it has become a trend to go to the IIT. Every year, 4 to 5 lakh students appear in the IIT entrance examination for 5000-6000 seats. The same is the case for administrative jobs, management courses after graduation and seats of medical colleges. There is nothing wrong in it but most of them do this without evaluating their strengths and get into depression. No one can stop you to appear in all these examinations but our education system is so rotten that a student is not in a position to get his proper evaluation done. Had there been a system of evaluation of strengths at individual levels, this mad race, the consequent depression and suicidal tendencies would have stopped.

No one seems to be really concerned with the basic issue that education must be received first. All people are more concerned with their political and economic gain.

In our life, we encounter personalities who are satisfied whatever they get and never think beyond that. In the books devoted to the development of self-motivation, you will read: in order to be stress-free, you should compare yourself with the individual who is of lower status than you. Do you think that such mentality is likely to lead you any where? It is correct that sometimes, you will not be able to do what you deserve but you should not do less than what you could.

One must compare himself with those individuals who are equal to him. Suppose that you are a school administrator. So you should analyze the success stories of people in your field, i.e., those who had started their career as teachers, became Principals and got a chance to launch their own institution over time, those institutions must have becomefamous. The analysis of such success stories of the personalities in the same field would give you clues. You compare such lines with your strengths; and if you feel that you also have that talent, there is no harm in following the same route.

Belive in fate but keep trying

Comparing yourself with the persons in other professions will not take you in the right direction, for the tips of success needed in other professions may not be useful in your profession. The resultant chaos, created due to the difference in profession will make you heavily stressed. Once you are stressed you loose fifty per cent of your strengths.

One day, I was watching breaking news on a news channel the news was that most corporate houses had employed astrologers to match the horoscope of the new entrants. These astrologers had tablet PCs to match the horoscope. They were of the opinion that a person having "Brihaspati and Shukra" (mythological names in Indian Horoscope) could not work under anyone as these signs are so called "Brahmins". These Brahmins were destined to control, so they could not be controlled. If you have a little knowledge of Indian mythology you would be able to infer that "Brihaspati and Shukra" are much below the ladder in the cabinet of God and they themselves are controlled by so many other planets.

Another factor plays a significant role in shaping the future of an individual. Some people call it fate. But remember that chance favours only those who have got a strong sense of commitment. Commitment reflects yours strengths. If you know that you are strong enough to complete a particular assignment, chance will favour you to achieve success. However, initiatives must be taken by you. There is a possibility that you may be reminded of your latent strengths by your well-wishers.

The important factor is that whether you know your strengths or someone else reminds you of the same, you can do only those tasks that your abilities would allow you to executive. So do not forget the balance mantra. You should not lose your happiness and achievements of the present by trying to achieve more in the future; if you do so, you would be over-duly stressed and lose your present too. It is correct that necessity is the mother of invention but, you must, read the biographies of famous inventors. They invented because they knew that they would be able to do that. They knew their strengths and utilized the same to achieve their target.

Chance will bring you near your target but it is you who has to shoot the target.

Here you are alone and success and failure is absolutely the result of your own destiny. The total sum of your physical and mental strengths will open the door of achievement for you. You should not hide your achievements as well as your failures. In the event of failure, you are not supposed to blame your destiny because by doing so, you are not going to achieve anything. Make it a point to own the failure and thank others. They may be your well-wishers and even your inner self for your success.

Worrying about or repenting over failure would give you disappointment and stress due to which you may loose another chance that may be knocking at your door and inviting you to avail the opportunity. You may console yourself that you thought of doing more than what you deserved. Wait for a while; evaluate the factors which are a hindrance in achieving your goal. Analyze what other strengths you need to achieve the goal. Now, reorganize your resources and fight for another chance. Nothing would stop you from going ahead as you are prepared yourself for the same.

Success brings happiness and failure brings dismay. We would be wrong in stating that failure pushes an individual towards success. The essence is that as soon as you recover from an unhappy situation, you would be able to cover some more distance towards your success which is your goal.

Luck is your worth. It favours only those who know their worth. You may be Hanuman but chances of getting a Ram for you would be remote possibility. In order to write your success story, your first task is to evaluate your own worth. You need not do more than your worth but you must utilize your worth completely to make you successful in your field.

Prove your individuality

Sri TN Sheshan reminded Indians that there is an office in New Delhi which is referred as "Office of the Chief Election Commissioner". This name became a myth in Indian democracy. History remembers those who have utilized there worth which they got from the Almighty. The story of Sri Rama Rao of Allore district of Andhra Pradesh is worth mentioning here. Belonging to the downtrodden caste of the Indian Caste System, he started life by begging on the streets. He received many setbacks in life. He hailed from a village. He knew his worth and decided to achieve success from the external sources, keeping these external factors fully controlled. Several NGOs tried to help him when he got fame but he wanted to be the master of his own destiny, choosing to do whatever he could do for his villagers and making his dream come true.

> **It does not matter whether you have the resources or not but it matters whether you have worth or not.**

It's the worth of the elephant which rakes in money worth lakhs even after its death. If you have all the resources for achieving something, and called "born with the silver spoon in mouth," what is your contribution to the society? The recipe of being successful with the help of motivating books can alter their image temporarily but their can never be image it permanent.

Even God, who has created this world, has not been able to image it else Lord Shankar would not have gone to jungle in order to save. Himself from the famous demon, Bhasmasur.

Time will pass and it will not come back again. Try to achieve the maximum of your worth in a limited period of time. There is no question of being unlucky. The only hitch is to start. Don't wait for some external force to make you move, the external force would be withdrawn, you would become stationary. Let your drive be your external force to pave the path for your success.

Believe in yourself

> **You must think that if you are not the best but you are better than all others who are with you.**

You must start believing in yourself. You must think that if you are not the best you are better than all others who are with you. You would be able to achieve according to your worth as you have already calculated your worth. Once this exercise is over, there is no need of thinking anything else, except dreaming for your success. You are not an ordinary person and once you start nurturing, this feeling, you would act in such a way that you would not commit mistakes. If you do, you would learn from them. Mistakes are committed by ordinary people. They are those people who are still in the preliminary stage of planning their success path. You are ahead of them, you have already covered a lot of distance committed mistakes. Now, you are leading towards perfection. You made mistakes. Hopefully, you learnt from them. In the present time you would not have been here. Somebody else would have taken your place. You have sharp mind and the decisions of sharp minds are also sharp. I don't think that you have the slightest doubt why am I saying all you would not have chosen to be successful.

I advice you to put a transparent cello tape on two words in your dictionary 'wrong' and 'mistake'. With a transparent tape on these words, they will not be visible easily and slowly you will forget these words. The person who does mistakes kills most of his time thinking how to rectify the committed mistake. Once you will commit no mistake you need not spoil your precious time. Hence, that saved time would be utilized for bringing your success closer to you.

Environment plays a significant role in shaping the career of a person. Plants and animal adopt themselves to the environment to save themselves from nature and predators. You are not alone on this earth. Success and failure are environment friendly words. You can compare achievements of Akbar the great with Ashok the great but you can't compare the success of Akbar the great with that of an individual. Your graph of success may move upwards in case you get the environment to work where people respect work and not the person and his connections. You know that generally, it does not happen. It is the environment that brands a person as successful or failed.

The example of Russi Modi best suits this context. The person who was the force behind the Tata's was the CMD of Air India. Russi Modi, regarded as a fiasco synonym of management in India was credited with being the most successful CEO of his decade. But the work environment of Air India did not allow him to use his learnt management concepts. Evaluation of this scene will help you to understand that basically, it was not Mr. Modi who had lost but certainly it was Air India that did not utilize his management expertise to become the best airline of the world.

With the advent of Liberalization, Privatization and Globalization (LPG) the environment factor has become most important. Previously, one had to compete against the natives only but now, one has to compete at the international level even if one is working in remotest corner in India. Here also, chance plays an important role that is called good break. It would lead you towards success. Success brings success but failures do not bring failures. People feel that only hard work is the key to success but I do not agree with this tenet. Hard work is one of many factors that lead you towards success. If hard work alone brings success, then a laborer, who works the whole day, would have been more successful.

Follow momentum equation

Sometimes, you will just be clicking and sometimes-you won't. That is okay. It is the cycle of life. When you are not clicking, plug away. When you are clicking, pour it on because momentum will help you to get larger gains in a shorter period with much less energy inputs. That is the momentum Equation!

When you are feeling good about how your work is going, ride the momentum and get as much out of it as you can! Don't imagine that whatever you do, the result would be according to your calculation. This should not happen, else you become an egoist and after that, your down-fall will start. Life always gives mingled results, not because it is its nature to give such results but because it has to give a balance to our life and career.

You must have observed the animals waiting for their prey. Sometimes, they go on waiting for the target till they finally achieve success. They also chase the target over long distance so that the latter ultimately gets fully exhausted. In case they fail, they take stock of the situation and search another prey. For us too, observation after a failure, in the midst of darkness, would give a ray of hope and by following that ray you would be able to consequr the world. The only condition is that during your worst days, when there is darkness all around you, keep your eyes open. That is only possible only if you control your tears. That is because tears close the eyes affecting the clarity of vision. Thus, there are chances of missing the forthcoming opportunities as well.

The path of success is not unidirectional but multidirectional, suggesting that getting a sign of "Road Closed," you immediately turn to get on the other road. In life, the road is not important but the journey is important. One has to run sometimes, walk fast, go slow, stop and follow all instructions to reach the destination. You should be more careful about your destination or goal. It should always be in front of you irrespective of your other commitments and busy schedules.

You should get motivated every day. Motivation may not always be positive. You must be careful in minimizing the effects of negative motivations. Sometimes you may get motivated to follow the shortcut method to achieve your target. Alternatively, you may think of achieving the same with the help of someone else. In any case, success would not be permanent as you did not have self motivation. It is equal to your worth multiplied by your zeal or perseverance. It is not present in any individual but it is the result of actions. Positive action generates positive motivation and negative action generates negative motivation.

Your thinking acts as the threshold of your motivation. This directionless motivation will lead you nowhere and you could be wasting your precious time too. This happens when you don't have a vision in your life. That is why you must have a vision for your life. A life without a vision is like a journey without a destination. If you have no idea of your destination, it is always advisable to wait and introspect to know or acquire a vision. It is not essential that one should always have a big vision but it is important to have a vision in proportion of your worth.

Remove fear of failure

> **The fear of failure is the biggest factor which holds anyone to move in the direction of goal achievement.**

You know your goal and you also know the path on which you have to travel to reach your goal. But distance and unknown factors could stop you from inching towards your destination. You should try to figure out the problems which you could encounter in case you are on your previously determined path.

A probability is there that your perceived difficulties may be there. But another probability is also there that you may not face any difficulty and your journey would be smooth. You must prepare yourself for goal-conducive and goal-annihilating probahilities. Experience would prove to be a good teacher in this context..

Problems, which you encounter in your life, make you perfect and they sharpen your decision making capability. This capability would be required even when you have become a successful individual.

You are unable to start a journey due to the fear that you may face some difficulties. However, this tenet is not justified at all. Till the time you are one of the individuals in the crowd no one would notice you but as soon as you are out of the crowd, all eyes of the crowd would be on you. Then, your every action, howsoever it may be, would be under scanner.

It is not that you do not know all these. You avoid this thinking that it would not happen to you. The happening or not happening of an event is not under your direct control. But you must foresee the mishaps to make yourself perfect. It may dodge you but you should not ignore it. Have you ever noticed creeper plants such as cucumber? They bear big fruits but without any support, they can't complete their life cycle. On the contrary, perennial plants take longer time to grow, give a large number of small-sized fruits and go on yielding fruits year after year. What's more, not a single part of a perennial plant is wasted when it die (due to natural causes). Think of being successful for ever than to achieve it for a limited period and you would be a laughing stock in your friendship circle. Any small permanent gain is better than a big temporary gain. The former relaxes and gives you an edge over others and always forces you to achieve better than the former one.

•

Chapter 2

Preserve Your Positive Energy

We know that energy is the capacity to do work. However, work can only be done if there is displacement. Without displacement, irrespective of the load you are carrying, you are not doing any work. Every action and reaction on this earth bears some cause-and-effect relationship. Energy applied on a person or situation to get a result in a desired way or direction may prove to be positive energy for you. Energy does not carry positive or negative signs but it is the person and the situation which makes it positive or negative.

Energy can be preserved and may be utilised at a later stage according to the need. Energy is a nonrenewable source and it must be utilised with care. The present war between the nations is for the possession of this energy only. The nation having the maximum source of energy is the most powerful one and so is the case with an individual. Matter can neither be created nor be destroyed but it can only be transferred from one form into another. Further, matter can be converted into energy. A form of energy can also be converted into another. In humans too, these concepts work. Every individual also has the potential energy according to his worth. For doing any piece of work, this positive energy gets converted to kinetic energy. Even when an individual is in deep sleep, he utilizes some of the energy for his Basic Metabolic Rate (BMR) which handles movements of body parts and operation of the heart during deep sleep.

An individual, who gets success in his life utilises his preserved potential energy up to the maximum to get the work done up to the level of his satisfaction.

Positive energy helps you cover the distance towards your goal whereas negative energy is mainly utilised in combating the forces that try to destabilize you. We may be able to overcome these forces with little imagination. However, most of us get entangled with these forces and waste our positive energy and time to show that we are not weak and can handle any situation. We must remember that our aim is not to handle those forces which stop our positive movement. We must learn to handle them carefully so that most of our energy may be utilised towards positive achievement of our goal.

Preserve positive energy

We should never pray for the problems to go away but pray for the courage and strength to overcome them in a positive way. I got this message from my friend. At the very outset, I felt that this is very good tenet. After reading this my daughter said, "Wow!" We must understand it fully.

Is it possible to have no problem in our life? I think it is not possible. If we are alive, then at every moment, there are activities and which lead to the generation of other activities. Every action has a reaction as a result, there is either a problem or happiness. In this world, we cannot remain isolated. We cannot operate in vacuum at any point of time.

Courage and strength are prerequisites for overcoming the problems we face. If we understand that every action or reaction is a problem, then we need the courage and strength to overcome them. Every action or reaction is a happening or misshapening. Deliberately or inadvertently, we may do an action or display a behaviour pattern. Hence, there would be a reaction in response to that action or behaviour.

My wife prepared the best breakfast using her culinary skills. Still, the quantity of salt was not perfect. Here, my reaction is very important. I could fire her and I may also get fired. Alternatively, she feel sorry, or she could show no reaction. In all the cases is it possible to maintain the harmony.....? The good atmosphere can be possible only when you have dignity and your mind is solution oriented. If you are solution oriented then you may add curd, salad or any food material to modify the combination of salt. Still you need to behave decently with your wife. In return your wife shall also be careful in future before using salt. In any case, this is a trial and error theory. To every action, there is a reaction. The moment your action is such that it improves atmosphere, the great moment starts. Happiness is inside not outside. We need to develop the art of devising solutions and producing happiness.

The quality of a person's life is in direct proportion to his commitment to excellence.

You must believe that you have all the talent to do whatever you want to. Note that everyone expects us to do our best. When we try to be the best, our actions converge to bring the best results for us. You may have done wrong actions but you have fair chances of improvement. If you have committed a mistake, it does not mean that you have lost all chances. At every moment, you get chance to improve the conditions. Depending upon your mistake and behaviour of others, you may need to do continuous efforts. Don't worry. Do your best and strive for the best output. Results will certainly be good. It may take some more time but final results would be favourable. Remember, every night ends with sun rays.

Don't remain suspicious and confused. Remain confident that always the best would happen. The only thing is that success may take some time to come you, this transpires due to reasons known or not known to us.

What we need to do is to do our best as per our competency and continuous hard working towards the goal. Then happiness, success and victory take care of your life and careers.

Be Confident

Confidence comes from knowledge. But knowledge itself does not create the art of its own implementation. You will certainly forget to implement the knowledge if you do not work hard on that knowledge. Implementation of knowledge requires hard work. One, who has patience as well as continuous vigil over developments and takes reasonable action as required, is sure to be a winner in his field. Excellence comes due to this art. You should strive to be the best human being. The Almighty created us as human beings and we should try to improve ourselves on a continuous basis. Those, who love human beings and nature, are the only ones who God loves. You can become a loving person if you master this art. Graceful success comes when you are having all these attributes i.e. hard work, knowledge, excellence and loving personality.

You should be careful about your behavior. Further, you must take care of your health too. Daily walking, jogging and yoga keep you fit. You should smile and laugh loudly, irrespective of your age. This can be possible only when you are a loving person. A person with heart full of grace and a soul oozing love can become a great man.

Material things do not bring permanent happiness. We must understand the management of balance of mind. We should have all material things which include car, bungalow, air conditioner, beautiful love unlimited financial resources etc. then also these things are only immediate rush of joy. After some time, all these material things would lead to depression, burden and frustration. It is very clear that all money in this world cannot buy happiness. Also, wealthy people are lonely and suspicious of other people's motives. Material things include money, fame, recognition, relationship, and recreation. Also, whose effect is only momentary.

Always be happy

Happiness is brought basically by the right mental attitude. One has to keep balance of his mind or attitude. One should understand the boundary of each thing. Every material thing has its own significance. Before trying to acquire them, we must evaluate them with cool mind. The evaluation of all these material things must be based on reasoning and not only on logic. Logic propels the mind in any direction where as reasoning propels it in the direction of positive thinking and finally leads to a satisfactory result.

Happiness comes when we admit where we are lacking and where we have to change ourselves. However, when we are reluctant to admit our needs because we're afraid that people might really reject us (which may create embarrassing situation), we become slave to all these needs and our actions become superficial.

Happiness comes to a person who is able to ask for help at the right time from the right person. Selection of the right person is very important. However, on many occasions, you don't know who the right person is. Even admitting our needs does not give a soothing outlet to our ego. Our needs and desires must create emotional and intellectual integrity so that people could trust us. People start going along with us hence we get tremendous self-esteem. The other alternative is to play games, put up a front, pretend to be something we are not and hope that no one will even catch us. This is the path on which we shall not get help we need. That is because we are on a false front and we pretend that we have no problems in our thinking. We need to remember that there is always somebody ready to help any body. Help does not always mean financial help. It may be advice, guidance etc.

There are lots of situations that have two extremes each. Examples are darkness or light, winning or losing, succeeding or failing, enthusing or depressing, happy or suffering, stronger or weaker. We can remain happy if we keep our attitude open towards positive things etc. If we wish to win we should behave nicely and our attitude should be like a tree bearing plenty of fruits. If we are loosing, then we should have the courage to think that this time will not last for ever. Sooner or later, you should solve the problem by having positive attitude and balanced vision.

What happens to good people when bad things happen to them? One out of such people could state, "I am going to remain cool, calm positive. I really want to do right things. I need help – I can't do it alone, Every one has problems but very few of us remain happy in adverse situations and those, who practice this theory of remaining cool even during adverse circumstances, are the real winners. All others go on searching the ingredients required to be successful.

Many years ago, there lived a Chief in North Africa. He was very rich and had many wives and children. But he was not happy. He thought, "I have everything but that does not make me happy. What must I do to be happy?

Once, he shouted angrily to his servants, "Why can't I be happy? What must I do to be happy?"

One of his servants said, "My Chief! Look at the sky! How beautiful the moon and stars are! When you look at them, you would see how good life is. That will make you happy.

"No! I have seen them but I am not happy," the Chief answered angrily. When I look at the moon and stars, I become angry. That is because that I know I cannot get them."

Then, another servant said, "My Chief! What about music? It makes man happy. We shall play music for you from morning till night; and it would make you happy.

The Chief's face became red with anger.

"No!" he cried, "What a silly idea!. Music is fine. However, I can't listen to music from morning till night, day after day.

So, the servants went away and the chief sat angrily in his room. Then, one of the servants entered into the room and bowed, "My Chief," he said, "I think I can tell you something that would surely make you very happy.

"What is it?" asked the Chief.

"It is very easy to do," said the servant, "You must find a happy man, take off his shirt and put it on. Then, his happiness will come into your body and you will be as happy as he would be!"

The Chief ordered to get such a person. Every one tried to search such a happy man but could not get any one. Hence even today the Chief is sitting unhappy even today scolding his servants.

Happiness is a state of mind. The day one understands this; one becomes the happiest person on this earth. The problem with us is that whenever something good happens, we congratulate ourselves and during adverse circumstances, we don't hesitate to blame everyone, except ourselves. We always spend most of our positive energy in clarifying to everyone that we are correct and all around us are wrong. What we are going to get from this exercise? Isn't it foolish on our part to be a sympathy seeker at all times? Such individuals never achieve anything in life and always try to find a scape-goat for their failure.

Dare to be successful

Success belongs to those who dare for undertaking ventures. If you lie below an apple tree and wait for an apple to fall automatically in your mouth, you would not be able to get any apple, the same thing happens in our life. We always wait for some miracle to happen that would catapult us to a platform higher than those of all others. We feel that we are the only one on this earth who deserves it. We must change this mental tendency or divine expectation.

We know that without hard labour, it is impossible to achieve anything in this world but we always go on waiting for some miracle to happen. The time we spend in waiting without a valid reason would never come again. On the other hand, far less time would be required to do the work methodically and get results.

There are people who always wait for the right time for everything and feel that, at very movement everything would move according to their calculation. When I started working on my first book, it was very difficult for me to concentrate. Like most of us, I also felt that the time for becoming a writer had not yet come. Days used to pass; I used to open my lap top and close it after sometime but no idea used to strike me to move on. One day, I decided to sit with my laptop for one year on a daily basis whether any idea struck me or not. I was amazed that it clicked and I finished my book in three months. I don't claim that it is a master-piece but whatever it is, it is the same thing which I wanted to produce. I feel satisfied now. It is also true that I took more than a year to get my book published after coming in contact with publishers, lI earnt how difficult they were.

The basic concept behind it is the same and that is commitment and not superficial involvement. Most of us get involve in any piece of work and very few of us get committed to one singal piece of work. Note that success favours these few individuals only. You decide to do something and start working in that direction by utilizing your all worth resources. If you are committed, you shall get the coveted result. You should not wait for the right time but that any time is right for the right piece of work is more than enough to push you to achieve your goal. The chances of your failure become less as you become more committed.

We fail to achieve what we deserve to get because of our own negligence. The role of external factors in failing us is negligible. Failure and success are due to our own thinking. We get results according to our own thinking.

Learn from other's mistakes

History does not give us any concrete and authentic examples to learn from. Babar, the founder of the Mughal empire in India, was a great warrior. He fought four battles during the four years of his tenure as the emperor of India. In all these four battles, he proved that he was a politician who came to India not to plunder but to establish the Mughal dynasty. If you have read Indian history, you must have noticed what a positive thinker he was. Before the start of the war, he used to assemble his soldiers and tell that they would not be able to return to their native land as it was far away. He used to add that if they die in the battle, they would go to heaven and if they won the battle, then India, which happened to be the richest country at that time, would be theirs. So the soldiers had no other alternatives, accept fight the battle and win.

History was shaped by the thinking of the rulers who ruled. Don't forget that self-help books and motivational trainers are not the product of recent times. Rather, they have been in vogue for so many years and would remain do in the year to come. There has always been unsuccessful and successful people in every decade and the conditions were also similar, except that previously success was much difficult than it is now. In this era, you are equipped with all modern scientific gadgets and technologies to make your path easier.

The only thing which has not changed and will never change is human psyche. It always varies with individuals. The stories of unsuccessful and successful individuals of the past and present are the same. Every individual, who fails, is not a committed individual and every individual, who wins, forgets everything and remember only that he must win. It is not a small matter but it makes all the difference. This difference is so significant that anyone would be able to see and observe it. If you want to be a winner, you have to know this difference.

One can't claim to be clicking always but when one clicks, he must click in the right direction. Clicking in the right direction means getting and doing the things towards our perceived goal. We can't change our goal as we are not clicking in that direction. It happens to everyone. Once you fix a goal and start working towards that goal, you would get a feeling that you have chosen a tough goal; and it will be difficult to get the result. It makes you think to change your goal. If you change your goal, you would be murturing a feeling of deserting the same and choosing some other goal.

While working with a group of teachers in a school owned and controlled by one of the biggest business houses, I was told by the HR manager of their establishment that they wanted a boost in the energy level of their teachers. The school was the oldest one in the state and was giving good results. Every year, three-odd students used to take merit positions in board examinations. I was told that last three-four years, the admission had been a low-ken affair as students are more interested in following a central syllabus. I was also told that the teachers were protesting for this switch-over and threatening to go on a strike if the process of switching over is not stopped immediately. After giving this set of information, the HR manager told me that if needed any other set of information he was ready to provide the same. I told him that I did not require anything else.

I sat with the staff over a cup of tea and told them what I had been briefed by the HR manager further added that they didn't need any session on positive energy. Rather they needed a session for eradicating their fears. They were surprised that I was changing my topic without making an assessment of their need. I convinced them that I would change my topic if it did not suit them.

I started the session and began analyzing the situation which could force them to go on strike. It was one of the toughest sessions of my career. I made up my mind to be a good listener. After an hour, discussion, it emerged that the school, being affiliated to state board, was an aided institution and receiving grant-in-aid from the government. The society used to give subsidies to compensate the difference. They were sure about their job, irrespective of the outcome. Their set-up was like any other government department. They were the best teachers of their respective subjects, they had long experience but were afraid of any appraisal of their performances during the past. They also lacked good language skills. Till date, they had been using their regional language and now, the requirement was of teaching through the English medium. It was really a problem and the management was unable to understand the same.

I came to know during course of the discussion that the goal was not clear to the management either. My first job was to finalise a goal in consultation with the irate teachers and the management representative. It also surfaced during discussion that previously, the subsidy given by the business house to the school was meager in comparison to their business revenue. Due to pay commissions report, the quantum of subsidy became huge and they were not in a mood to the part with such a huge sum of money.

I was able to diagnose the problem. Until present, everyone was working with symptoms only the society wanted to go with the time of providing modern and better education but the staff wanted to maintain the status quo. I was supposed to get my job completed as a consultant up to complete satisfaction of both parties.

Determined to get the result

Once you are determined to achieve a result, you feel that the conditions which were opposing you to get the result turn in your feavour. It happens due to your determination. I took the issues one by one and assured them of their secured jobs. I assured them in writing that their jobs were secure. But I also mentioned some terms and conditions on which they were working with an assurance to get trained to suit to the new system within six months (with full commitment). The only option open to me was to be a deserter which I did not want to become. It was my positive energy which moulded the situation in my favour. I knew that to prove myself as better than others, I would not get a second chance.

Sometimes, nature also tries to test you to make sure that success is going to the right hands. Being a successful individual, you are on the top of the decision making tree; and any failure from your side can cost you dearly. It is your self-respect which respects the self of others. A person having low self respect can't respect the complete self of others. He would go on bringing down the self-respect of others, privately or publicly, as he has no idea what its result is going to be.

You must understand that life will always bring problems to you and you have to go on sorting the same on a daily basis. If you manage to sort out small problems, there is no doubt that you would also manage to sort out the biggest problems you might face in life. Everyone goes on solving problems on a daily basis. Sometimes, it is just a reflex action which does not require a good brain-storming and becomes routine. Sometimes, we have to devote time and energy to get a solution. In both cases, our abilities are under acid test and there are fifty-fifty chances of losing or gaining in the end.

We keep on evaluating those who are around us, on a daily basis, for knowing some details about them. It is a normal human psychology. It happens as we want to prove that we are better than them by knowing them well. Unfortunately, in doing so, we forget that the other person is also doing the same thing. Had we forgotten everything and everyone and done as per our best capabilities, we would have proved ourselves better than most of others. Remember that by making one smaller we don't become bigger than one.

Every individual's worth and capabilities are a unique gift and they are not comparable to any one, not even to his near and dear ones. The performance of the individual is also unique. It was the unique thinking of Picasso, Newton, Lincoln and others which made them different from others. In fact, it is true for all successful people.

If that is the condition, what is there to know about others, good or bad? It is not going to help you in any way. You are required to enhance your own capabilities and competencies to make yourself unique. You must understand that the progress of the world is the result of unpopular decisions. The decisions which can be deduced by others and yourself cannot be unique. How would you get appreciation, even money, if you are taking some decisions just like others are doing. Appreciation is the result of uniqueness which can't be copied.

The progress of the world is the result of unpopular decisions.

People state that they can learn to be successful. I disagree with this theory that there is any readymade rule to become successful. I am sure that there are rules to become a failed person. In order to be a successful, you have to think and produce something unique, much above the thinking of others who are in competition with you. It is this uniqueness which makes someone popular as people feel that the individual is different from the crowd.

In order to produce or do something unique, one need not require high IQ or EQ. The requirement for doing something different from others is one's zeal, initiative and commitment to do the task in question. Sitting ideal and thinking without any action does not produce any result.

Take timely action

Time is an important factor for realizing any innovation. A number of persons think on the same line, very few out of them make a start and very few of them chase the goal. Remember the person behind Bisleri. Even today, you will not find this word in any dictionary. He thought of selling normal water at a rate which was a Herculean task in India. In our country, seventy per cent of population is below poverty line. He thought, planned an action and implemented the action. Today, more than hundred brands of packed water are there but Bisleri has its uniqueness.

MS Oberai was a simple clerk. He had a vision and consequently, he became successful in establishing Oberai chain of hotels. The son of the an ordinary father, KK Patel became successful in outshining brands like Hindustan Lever through his "Nirma" washing powder. It is now the maximum selling brand of washing powder in India. Topiwala came to Mumbai with a hundred-Rupee note and his matriculation certificate. He too had a vision to achieve a turnover of five crore Rupees every year in the business of Bindi, used on the forehead of ladies. Dr. Sarad Kumar Dikshit got heart attack twice and the lower part of his body does not work properly. His vocal chord has been taken out. But he completed forty five thousand surgeries free of cost.

Another unique example is that of Beethovan; the greatest music composer was deaf. Albert Einstein was a simple clerk who later became the famous scientist of the world. Gola Mair was a simple school teacher and became the prime minister of Israel. Franklin D

Roosevelt was sick and after becoming the president of USA, both of his legs got paralyzed. He is remembered as the famous statesman of the world.

It is your commitment towards your goal which pushes you towards success.

In India, we discuss the example of Dhiru Bhai Ambani. He had established the biggest business empire and earlier than that, was a petrol pump collection agent. Ms. Mayawati, a simple primary school teacher, became the chief minister. She became the inventor of a new term Social Engineering. I am sure, the way this social engineering is working and giving the results, that time is not far away when we will see another iron lady becoming the prime minister of our country. She may be better than the former lady prime minister of India.

I am not stressing that nothing is impossible in this world but I want to tell you that nothing is impossible if commitment is there. Your commitment forces you to achieve the target. It does not allow you to take rest and have a sleep till you achieve. It may be a negative goal also but that is also a commitment. The best example of negative commitment is of Osama bin Laden. If negative commitment can go up to such an extent, you can presume what will be the results if this commitment is positive.

Nothing is imposible if their is commitment.

Empower yourself

Positive energy charges you with unlimited strength to get the work finished. You should wish to achieve something, be ready to fight the problems coming your way, have a fire to achieve the same and see the result. There is nothing on this earth which will stop you to achieve the same. It's not that you will get that as a gift but you really deserve the same.

The examples of successful people, who were born without a silver spoon in their mouth, are numerous; everyone has a separate story to tell. Success is a solo song presentation and not a chorus. Remember, only "old age" strikes an idle man who does not want to do anything. No pushing is going to help an idle man if he is exhausted and the battery of his life is over. He takes failure as his fate whereas he is only person to be blamed for this end. No one can give you anything in charity.

I remember that I had put forth a proposal to the Indian representative of the UNICEF for one free meal during interval in schools to attract in primary schools while working with the District Primary Education Project in Bihar. It was due to the fact that with all interventions still a large number of students were out of school in primary classes. The UNICEF representative, an Indian, flatly refused the proposal and was critical in remarking that by giving donation we would not be able to eradicate poverty. He cites the examples of several nations to prove his points and there was no doubt that everyone sitting in that meeting was convinced.

We can change if we are ready to change.

Newton's second law of motion states that the rate of change of momentum of a body at rest is directly proportional to the applied force and the change takes place in the direction of the applied force. This theory is true for our life also. We can change if we are ready to change and without this, readiness external force would be able to change our state of mind. The readiness is a self-propelled action and it has to be initiated within ones' own-self without taking any extra intervention. If it is due to any external intervention the chances of coming to rest is always there after the removal of the external intervention.

The desire of doing something special is really unique. Every one perceives this desire but it is unique in the sense that only a few of them go on igniting this desire to make it a burning fire. Once the fire has been ignited, the individual goes on moving towards his goal and never comes to rest without achieving the same. You can also find a number of examples in which people started with a unique idea but deserted the same idea in the middle. Hence, they failed to achieve anything.

Qutubuddin Aibak, the greatest king of the slave dynasty, perceived the idea of constructing the 'Qutub Minar' and started working on that idea. He worked on it up to his death. Although he was not able to complete his dream project during his life-time, his project was completed by Iltutmish, his son-in-law. This is commitment. Once you are committed to an idea, you will not take rest till you complete the task in question. An idea is an idea till it is with you. Remember, if you want to kill an idea, discussed it in a meeting. This meeting includes outsiders as well as your near and dear ones.

As soon as you conceive an idea, people around you start criticizing it; this goes on till nothing is left intact. They do it, thinking that you are unnecessarily utilizing them to make yourself unique. It also happens as they are not sure whether the idea would click or whether you would be successful or not. Had the inventors and successful people made this mistake of discussing their ideas, they would not have achieved what they achieved.

The success of KK Patel was his uniqueness. Had he discussed the idea of launching a washing powder in front of an MNC like Hindustan Lever that had worldwide name and fame, people would have persuaded him not to venture into this business. Then, we would not have seen another brand like Nirma in the markets. It is the story of most people who dared to think slightly different.

No one appreciated me when I thought of writing something and getting it published. My own kith and kin started demoralizing me, saying that writing a book was not a joke and that one had to be creative. In the beginning, I also felt that it would be a futile experiment to write. One had two hours in the evening and decide to utilize that free slot. I thought that if, my work could not be published, I could to get it published in journals. In order to test my writing, I sent some of my articles to journals like HRD. When a few of them got published, I became sure that I was moving in the right direction.

The story did not end here. More than twenty publishers rejected my first manuscript. Three of them rejected it after completing all formalities like getting a contract signed on the stamp paper and keeping me waiting for more than a year and finally, rejecting the manuscript. But I was also adamant. I kept on writing, thinking that if I did not get it published during my lifetime my kids might be able to get it done after my death. I had learnt that so many rejected manuscript had been published after the death of the writers and became best-sellers. Another parallel thought also forced me to continue with my work. It was that it would be a good reading for me when I would be unable to move my fingers on my laptop. Today, my third book in the series is in your hands. I do not claim that my books have been in the category of best sellers but the fourth and fifth reprints of my two books arrived in just two years in the market.

I am not trying to stress that my writings were superb or that the publishers returned my books due to enmity with me. You think and list out the consequences. If the consequences are within your tolerable limit, you are advised to start immediately and you shall to be successful in your venture. This is called calculated risk taking. One must take calculated risk if one wants to achieve something in life.

Only two types of people fail the first category comprises of those that go on thinking and do not do anything and the second who go on doing anything without thinking.

One should believe in going upstairs by leaving one's footprints on every stair. If you are not leaving anything unattended, you are satisfied. Keep pace with your energy. People reach the top jump and leave the stairs. There is no harm in doing so but remember that we are interested in taking calculated risk. The potential of taking calculated risk varies from one individual to another and would be proportionate to time and other factors.

There are runners who use their potential in the beginning to leave everyone behind but are unable to reach the finishing points for want of energy. That is because they had consumed all energy in a bid to reach the top. Such a runner receives applause in the beginning which charges him to do better and better but as soon as someone else pushes him back his positive energy starts diminishing in the same proportion. Hence, applause is also not there. Applause is always and will be always for winners. The winner in any game is the individual and the team that maintains its pace.

We notice that a number of individuals around us start work with dedication and great speed but suddenly, after sometime, their speed as well as dedication starts diminishing. There can be two reasons behind this phenomenon. Firstly, these could be wrong goal selection for which they might not be committed and second may be their versatile nature. They start any work by copying others but are unable to maintain the pace to complete the work either for want of the positive energy or for want of concentration. One can be a winner only if he knows fully what he is doing and what would be his worth after completing the task. If any of these factors is not correct, the chances of being successful are very little.

Be firm in action

Success is not a one-time game but a continuous endeavour. An individual, who has the patience of undertaking such endeavour, can taste the fruit of success. You will be amazed to know that all of us have this success motive but only few of us try in the direction of its achievement. While trying to achieve a goal, one must

understand the result of one's knowledge and not the result of one's learning speed. Learning speed is a learnable quality which one can learn while working on it.

Your priority should be to do the best in the direction of your goal and not to always think about it. Any piece of work done with commitment shall certainly bring result. The question may be of time. You would find an individual who gets result with less effort whereas there would be an individuals who need some extra efforts to get the same result. Nevertheless, the result shall come. I was discussing with my favourite and the most respected teacher the difference between an intelligent and weak student. He came up with an answer which was funny but afterwards, he proved his funny answer to be correct. According to him, an intelligent student forgets his subject matter five minutes after the examination whereas a weak student forgets his answer five minutes before the start of the examination.

IQ is a good measure for testing the intelligent of man. However, I do not agree with the concept that the persons with high IQ levels would be good decision makers working with a number of individuals, I concluded that the decision making capacity of the mediocre people is superb. The intelligent people get a number of solution for a problem as they are blessed with the better thinking capacity. They are adapt at utilizing their neurons (the brain cells used for thinking). But they hesitate a lot to implement any one of the alternatives due to the fear of failure. I do not hesitate in saying that intelligent individuals are more concerned about their image than about finding a solution to a problem.

You can't do right things without doing wrong ones. If you can you are superb. I believe in the theory that those people who do not do anything, never commit mistake. There are aircraft crashes and we are aware of the same. Sometimes, they occur due to some terrorist activities but most of the times they occur due to human errors. But it does not mean that we should park all aircraft in hangers. In India, there are the maximum number of deaths due to snake-bites and that is because most Indians have the habit of walking bare-foot. But it does not warrant killing all snakes who are the preservers of our ecosystem.

The people who do not do anything never commits mistake.

For the fear of committing mistakes one should not avoid taking decisions as it will lead stopping our progress and after sometimes we will be left with a situation where no decision is required. We must remember that a good decision is the result of several bad thoughts and these bad thoughts may not only generate in the individual having low IQ but it equally gets generated in the individuals having higher IQ. In order to be successful you require only moderate intelligence. Even Chetan Bhagat has also endorsed the same thinking.

For success perseverance is more important than intelligence. You can not claim that an intelligent individual will be successful but you can claim any time and any where that a person having perseverance is surely going to be successful. Perseverance is your worth and you can't deny your worth if you are true to yourself. Each and every individual on this earth gets equal and fair chance of being successful.

In India IAS (Indian Administrative Service) is treated as the most respected service and the people in this service are known as the most intelligent individuals being selected through the top selection board of the country. I am not denying the same but think for a situation. Most of the intelligent students go to IIT and medical after completing their plus two examinations (please note, I am not telling all but "most" only). But this "most" comprises of nearly 90% of the students. After completing their technical degree in engineering or medical few of them again try to be an IAS but the number is not so which makes a significant difference to deny the fact.

> **You must understand clearly that you will never get anything without committing any mistake**

All professions are rewarding

Success is not a one-time game but a continuous process; and it goes to the individual who believes in committing mistakes. You must understand clearly that you would never get anything without committing any mistake. The individual who do not hesitate in committing mistakes, is sure to be a successful individual but the condition is that he should not repeat those mistakes. Bismarck believed that people should learn from the mistakes committed by others, as life may not give enough chances to commit mistakes and learn.

I remember the lady teacher who approached me after completing a training session. She asked that she never wanted to be a teacher because she always stood first in the university in her subject. She tried twice to be an IAS but did not get a chance. This pushed her into a state of depression and to kill her time, she had joined this teachings profession. I listened to her carefully and concentrated on only the statement– she became a teacher to kill her time. I thought what a mistake most of us commits thinking that we are killing the time but it is just opposite; time is killing us!

I tried to convince her that the teaching profession is not bad and there are always chances to prove one's worth in one's profession with a condition that one should be ready for that. She was frustrated, as she used to be compared with the teachers having third division. That was the main reason of her frustration. That is why she was not getting selected for IAS. I took nearly three sessions with her on bringing her to understand that every profession has huge growth possibility for any individual who wants to grab opportunities.

I gave her the examples of persons who had earned name and fame in this profession only because they had devoted themselves to their respective professions and not even thought of anything else. I also gave her an example that was not directly related to the teaching profession but fit for the situation. Nearly five years ago, the Government of Rajasthan decided to ply hi-tech Volvo buses on NH 8 from Delhi to Jaipur. It was decided that they would not recruit new drivers but shall select the drivers from the existing poor of drivers who were running the government-run buses on this route. They invited applications and out of nearly three thousand applicants, thirty-six got selected. They were the drivers who had little knowledge of Volvo buses. They got the important and guidance from the drivers of Volvo buses that carried tourists from Mumbai to Jaipur and Delhi as these Volvo buses were plying, at that time, on the Mumbai-Poona highway. During their journey, while stopping on the road side hotels, the drivers of Rajasthan State Transport Corporation, who were enthusiastic about these buses, used to have conversation about these buses. However, their other friends were busy killing their time in unnecessary discussion or playing cards.

At the efficient utilization of time has brought about complete change in these drivers. After getting selected to drive Volvo buses. They were able to drive such buses. Their salary become five times the existing package. The perks were raised too. So, there are chances of growth in every profession, irrespective of its worth. Individuals doing quality work are always needed and they would always be less in supply than demand.

I did not get the time to meet the lady for nearly five years but when I saw her during the course of a training programme at the Indian Institute of Management (Ahmedabad) organized by the Central Board of Secondary Education for its principals, I found her a changed individual. Your view makes the world. Change it and the world shall get changed. Your view is your destiny. The destiny is in your hand as only you can change your views and none else, irrespective of as many training sessions you may go through. Training session can only put you on a thinking process.

It is not that people are not ready to change their views we are changed for a few moments but we go back to old routine. The same happens to us when we are in a training session on positive thinking or going through a book on this subject. Till the time we are with the book, we assure ourselves to change but as soon as that external factor is removed, we turn to our original thinking process and claim that the training session or the book was useless.

Your view makes the world. Change them and the world will get changed.

One can't mould all people of the world according to his view but one may change one's view to suit the most.

A king had a daughter and he loved her more than anything in the worlds. In order to keep her daughter safe from any distress, he sent her to a foreign country known for its beauty and splendid structures. The roads were clean and smooth. He never called her daughter to meet him but used to go to see her.

Once the daughter wanted to come to her own native land but this news gave sleepless nights to her father. He was worried about the condition of roads in his capital. He was unable to find the solution. How her would daughter walk on these roads, full of stones. She would get hurt and the king can't tolerate even a little trouble for his daughter.

Next morning, the king came to the court and looked disturbed. The prime minister came to know the reason and was not convinced with the king's solution for making all those roads smooth where the princess was supposed to go. It was a tedious task. All other developmental works had to be stopped to complete this.

He advised the king to put a special type of material tied to the feet of princess, as shoes had not been invented till that time. The prime minister said that the princess would be able to wear some cover on her feet to walk around. That way, her feet would not get hurt.

The king liked the idea and was happy with the valuable suggestion given by his minister.

We must understand that it is easier to change ourselves to achieve something than to change everyone who has nothing to do with our achievements. In management, it is always advised to adjust according to the organization, as the organization shall never adjust according to the thinking of an individual.

Once you try to change your views, it is sure that most of your problems would be eliminated. Thus, you would be relieved of so many adverse consequences.

•

Chapter 3

Get Motivated Everyday

In the valley of river Brahmputra, there lived six men. They were blind. Once, they had an argument over how the elephant looked. They decided to go and find out an elephant. They were taken near a domesticated elephant and told to see the elephant.

The first blind man went near the elephant and touched its broad side. Then, he said, "The elephant is like a hard, rough and plastered wall." The second blind man held one of its tusks and declared, "I bet the elephant is like a roller." The third blind man approached the elephant and touched the tail. He said; Both of you are wrong. The elephant is very much like a rope."

Now, it was the turn of the fourth blind man. He touched the elephant's trunk. He shouted "Fools, all of you!" The elephant resembles a reptile. "The fifth blind man touched the elephant's ear. He blurted, "The elephant almost looks like a fan." The sixth and last blind man touched the leg of the elephant and declared, "The elephant is like a strong heavy pillar." The dispute never ended for every blind man was visualising a part of the elephant as the whole.

Our life, with all its ups and downs, is looked differently by different individuals, even by our near and dear ones. Sometimes, we feel that we would have been better, had we have done this or that. But the question is. who stopped you from doing that? You are the master of your destiny. In case something that did not strike your parents for your sake, why did you not take it? Why should you weep over the spilt milk? Most people on this earth feels that they did not get what they deserved but very few of them realize that it was done due to their own mistakes and that no one was responsible for it.

It is always advisable to get the best and not to compromise with anything less than the best. This can happen only when you get motivated everyday by a positive motivational reinforcement. This reinforcement will play a vital role for your positive thinking process. Positive thinking is the precursor of success; and you can never imagine anything to happen in your life without having a positive reinforcement.

Ninety five per cent of your emotions are determinedby how you interpret events.

Ninety five per cent of your emotions are determined by how you interpret events. Your thinking shapes your future action. Any action would certainly lead to a reaction, whether you like or not. The reaction is the direct result of your action. If the action is positive, the reaction would be also positive and the vice-versa is also true. You must try to do a positive action in order to get a positive reaction.

Positive thinking is the balanced diet of the brain whereas negative thinking leads to the malfunctioning your brain. We must avoid of negative thinking to enter our brain it can never create environment for your success. An individual, who thinks of defeating someone has negative thinking and would not be able to defeat anyone, as he is being pulled in the opposite directions. An individual, who works hard to win, is certain to win irrespective of many hindrances coming his way. That is because he is charged with positive energy to tackle all situations.

Thinking is a learnable behaviour and with regular practice, one can master the art of thinking. Try to see the bright side of any situation or any event. Don't think that a tumbler is half-empty; think that it is half-full. You may feel that it is easy to preach than practice. You may be correct also but why should you copy an individual who does not practise what he preaches? Start learning the art of inculcating positive thinking from such individuals as practice what they preach.

You can't dream a rose without a thorn but you never pluck a thorn when you pluck a rose.

In our daily life, we come across a number of people who we don't like. You must remember that on this earth, there is nothing which can be termed as scrap. Everything living or nonliving has its own importance. It is our thinking which makes something important and something else useless. You can't dream a rose without a thorn but you never pluck a thorn when you pluck a rose. In the same way you would never find an individual who doesn't have a single good quality. Our intention should be to get and assimilate the qualities which are important and useful to us and leave those which are of no use to us. Avoid liking and disliking people.

Your attitude shapes your behaviour and your behaviour shapes your actions. Your action brings positive or negative results for you. Make sure to think positively from the very beginning to get a positive result only. It is also a learnable behaviour and with a regular practice, it is not difficult to get the result that is desired. You should be the master of your thoughts.

Go for day dreaming

Dream is the precursor to success. Dream does not mean the dream which we visualize through our sub-conscious mind (when we are in deep sleep). Rather it denotes daydreaming which we visualize when we are in a super conscious state. It is a dream which an individual perceives when he is fully conscious and sometimes, it is called "building castles in the air." The "tree house" at Udaipur in Rajasthan is an example of such a dream. I came, saw and conquered is the famous statement of Julius Cesar. It signifies the idea of perceiving something and moving to achieve the same with commitment.

> **Most of us have a habit of daydreaming and it is not a unique characteristic; rather the uniqueness lies in chasing the dream.**

Most of us have a habit of daydreaming and it is not a unique characteristic; rather, the uniqueness lies in chasing the dream. Sitting in a multiplex and watching a movie, most people in the audience dream to have a wife resembling the heroine who is in front of them on the screen. There is no harm to have such dreams. But as soon as they come out of the theatre, they even do not bother to remember anything. So, the dream was so transitory that it vanished when the visual effect (movie) was withdrawn.

It is not daydreaming but hallucination. Majority of us are the victims of hallucination. Only eyeing something would never bring a result or fulfill our wish unless we put our tireless efforts to achieve the same.

Today, the increased rate of depression and suicidal tendencies in youth are a result of this very hallucination.

We want to have everything what we desire. If we don't get the same, we start blaming our luck. It seems that luck is an individual who chooses to bestow his gift to any Tom, Dick and Harry. In reality, it does not happen. One has to pay the price for having something in this world. Desire is not going to fulfill your appetite. You have to collect the ingredients and assemble them according to the nature's recipe and cook the same by putting in your best efforts. Then the chances are there to get a good dish.

Do you need four arms. Deduce after going through this story.

There was a woodcutter, who used to earn his livelihood by cutting trees in a jungle and selling wood in the market. One day, early in the morning, he left for the jungle, sharpened his axe and tried to fell a small tree. Suddenly, he heard a voice, "Stop. If you will spare my dwelling place, I will give you boon."

"Who are you? Are you God?" asked the woodcutter hung on the tree.

"I am an elves and I am empowered to give boons at my discretion", replied the entity.

The woodcutter thought that it would be better to consult his wife before asking for the boon. Thus, he requested the elves to give him a day's time. The elves agreed.

The woodcutter and his wife discussed but they couldn't reach any conclusion. They decided to take the advice of their friend.

The friend replied, "Why are you not asking for four hands in place of two? It would help you earn twice the amount that you are earning with only two hands."

The woodcutter got convinced and asked the elves for the same boon. He had four hands with one head now. On that day, he really cut more wood than he used to cut on a normal day. Thinking that he would earn some extra money and how it was going to be spent, he moved towards the market place. Suddenly, he saw himself surrounded by a group of people. Upon seeing his four arms, they thought that he was a devil and killed him.

Unusual demands lead to unusual endings. The examples of the successful people around you would prove this theory. None of them was born with a silver spoon in his or her mouth. It was their will-power which was with them as their best motivator. It was not a planned journey for them but they solved the problems on the way and got results. One thing, which was common in most of them, was the desire of achieving something better than others.

They dreamed and went on analyzing their dreams to start a movement in the direction of their goal attainment. It was not their destiny but they made it their destiny and shaped it according to their desire and worth. It is not important who dreamed first but it is important to know who started first. It is your attitude of perceiving anything that makes a difference.

Attitude and personality are as important as experience and ability.

Change your attitude

Attitude and personality are as important as experience and ability. Choose wisely and act according to your worth. Attitude is the building block of your success storey. The man, who has a positive attitude has an edge over the person who has a doubt. You rub your two hands. It is certain that you will feel some heat irrespective of how weak and old you are. The heat is not coming from outside but it is the biological energy of your body which is always within you.

You have to feel the heat. It is the basic rule of nature. You start doing something positive and it is certain to get a positive result. In mathematics, basic rules of various concepts like algebra and trigonometry point out to the same conclusion– positive results through positive inputs and calculations and negative results through negative inputs or calculations. In the same way, positive thinking generates only positive results and at any point of time. You can't get a negative result with pure, positive inputs and efforts.

It is not that you are reading something new here but it is that you are being reminded of to start using your latent potentials. It is never too late to visualize it. The day you start will be your D-day and you are sure to do better than those who may have started earlier than you. It is the commitment which makes the difference, as most people are only involved, not committed. Involvement always gives mediocre results and one can't achieve the best with just involvement.

Your attitude would make all the difference. Going to a doctor for consultation, with broken attitude may not bring you relief, as in the beginning, you may have a doubt about the capability of the doctor. You should never doubt your attitude, as it is the propelling force for you. At any point of time, you should not imbibe an idea of playing with words without thinking about the consequences. Most of us do this just to give an impression to others about our attitude and beliefs which, in reality, we don't possess.

Your reality would shape your attitude. Having positive attitude towards everything paves your way to success. Till you are positive in your thinking you would not be successful.

> **Your attitude is an expression of your values, beliefs and expectations. Your attitudes shape your values and you act according to your value system only.**

Your attitude is an expression of your values, beliefs and expectations. Your attitude shapes your values and you act according to your value system only. Positive attitude inculcates positive values and negative one gives rise to broken and shaken value system A disturbed value system forces, you to achieve anything by utilizing any method, whether it may be right or wrong.

Only a few of us avoid the temptation of availing wrong methods to achieve their goal but in case they achieve that, it is not going to last longer.

Attitude and confidence level can take you forward or backward. It is the attitude that matters. It is as important as your expertise or knowledge. Don't ever let negative feelings overtake you or come near you. Always say to you, "I shall do my best and succeed." Any negative suggestions adversely affect your attitude. Remind yourself that if you do not succeed, expectations sometimes tempt you to adopt unfair means. Keep in mind that occasionally, it is natural to fail in any venture but never as a human being.

A right approach with the right attitude and a strong value system shall ultimately lead you to success and goal. Always stay calm and make yourself comfortable while trying to tackle any problem. Study your problem carefully before attempting to overcome it. Attempt the easier part first. It would give you confidence to tackle the difficult part later.

You have to decide whether you are right or wrong. You are the only 'judge' to judge the same. There is nothing right or wrong, except place and time. Suppose you are in a queue to purchase the ticket and you bribe someone to get an early chance, it is a wrong step. If you are in a hospital with an accident victim who is unknown to you and you bribe someone there to get early treatment, according to me, you are not wrong here. It is the situation which makes you do right or wrong and the things you will do remain with you forever. In the present time, you may not be able to know the implications but in due course of time, results will remind you of your wrongdoings.

You must have noticed some individuals who go on abusing the system or consider some others as the major factor for their failure. Think for a while. In case any individual can make you to fail, he deserves the best and not you as he is better than you. A good driver is not who drives well but the one who saves his vehicle from a driver who is not so good (but is on the road with him in the a race). When you are trying to get the best, you should be careful towards everyone and every situation. You are trying to get the best and you have to prove that you deserve the best, irrespective of all the odds.

Attitude and confidence level carry you forward or backward. It is the attitude that matters. It is as important as your expertise or knowledge.

Don't care for everyone

You would always have a set of people everywhere who would be critical about you. You can't give a blind look to these people. If you don't care at all what anyone else thinks less about you, you would perform differently because of the stress generated in your mind. This decision shall shape your future course of actions as well.

Once, two frogs fell into a well. The passing by the well frogs looked down and started "Oh dear! You have fallen into a deep well and would not be able to come out." They started crying. One of the frogs in the well listened to this, lost all hope and gave up all efforts to come out of the well. The other frog was deaf. He thought that the other frogs were encouraging him to come out of the well. He gathered all his strength and with a powerful jump, he came out of the well.

Sometimes, giving a deaf ear to your criticism helps you achieve the best. I was working with one of the biggest industrial houses of India on their educational project. My friends would tell me about those difficulties which I would be encountering. Most of my friends are working as school and college principals and are satisfied. Whenever we meet, everyone criticizes the school management on the plea indifferent to their demands for doing something good to students. It was not restricted to only privately managed institutions.

Rather, it was the case for society and government-run educational institutions as well.

I was never part of such discussion but they can't avoid talking to me either. I was not critical of any of their arguments, except when they used to say that they did so many things, brought the institution to a height and still the management did not have belief in them. At this juncture, I used to ask them whether they did it as a social service or were they paid for the job." Sometimes, I also suggest to them to change the organization once they are not feeling happy but till date, none of my friends changed their organization.

It was not that I never faced any problem in my organization; it happens to every one, irrespective of one's designation and the height in the organizational chart. But never forget that you are being paid for the same. I am of the opinion that in any organization, your commitment is up to the level of putting all facts to your superiors and if still they want something to be done in a particular way, implement the same, forgetting what is right and wrong. In case you don't agree with me, the best way is to have a friendly exist. Don't be in tension because you would not be able to deliver the best and loose the image which you may have built in years.

You have enough courage and strength to face any unwanted situation. Once you are dissatisfied, you may take wrong decision and become biased. Your actions shape your personality. Your personality works at your work place. The people around you take you as a person in the way they perceive your personality.

The self-esteem of people plays a vital role in shaping their personality.

The personality traits of successful people are not something special but it is shaped by their actions. Self-esteem of people plays a vital role in shaping their personality. You perceive something and act in that direction and that gets imbibed in your personality. It is your sum total and most of us can't action or learning there of hide our actual personality traits. No one would be able to give negative traits to your personality, except yourself.

Success and failure are comparative terms. A successful person may not be treated as successful by someone else. It simply signifies that you need not worry about others for your success story but you have to satisfy yourself, keeping the natural laws as a benchmark. Bench-marking is important, as it compares you with some norms. You have to decide your own benchmark and work to come up to it.

Avoid criticising

Most of the time, I feel why most people try to know others, not themselves. Knowing someone better may give you a feeling of relaxation that the person is inferior to you, or you may get tense, knowing that the person is superior to you. In any case, it is not going to give you anything till you learn sometime from the person. But we don't hesitate in learning about anyone, whether it is essential or not.

I love to travel by train and given a chance, I would never fly. But most of the times, the restriction of time only does not allow me to travel by train. I travel to different places and I can vouch that every Indian is the same irrespective of his place of birth and language. During the recent past, many events happened that gave hints about regionalism. But I have a strong belief that it is this nature which makes every Indian united. They may speak different languages and their eating habits may vary but they think alike. Most of them don't want to work but would go on criticizing any person or the system in spite of having a little or no knowledge about the situation or the person in question.

Most Indians get a job, marry, have one or two kids, buy a dwelling unit and a four wheeler and the life ends here. They are contended with their family and least bothered about anything. It leads us nowhere, and we still have a feeling that we are the best. They have enough time to watch a three-hours movie or to spend three-hours in front of TV but they hardly have enough time to move out and understand the woes of others. That is why in our country, the government jobs are treated as the best as it does not demand anything extra.

In our country, experience is always one multiplied by the number of years and one is never added the number of years in service. In the former case, you are just multiplying your gained experience of one year till you are on the job where as in the second one, you are gaining something new every year. The second condition is a bit difficult, as you have to be continuously innovative in your job and that requires your time. The problem is that most of us don't have time for this.

We have branded our politics as a bad game and that too, without playing the game.

We have all rights to abuse our politicians and we have branded our politics as a bad game and that too without playing the game. Actually, we have accepted our defeat without playing the game, as we don't feel ourselves competent to play this game. It is not that we are born deserters but over the years, we start behaving like that. We believe that politics is a game of bad people but we forget that by thinking, so we are indirectly abusing our freedom fighters without who, we would not have become a free nation.

It is not that we are born bad but our thinking has deteriorated. We always see everything in suspicion as we are being trained like that. Since morning, till we retire to bed, we listen only to negative news and instructions. It is better to instruct our kids not to believe every one but it does not mean that all individuals on this earth are bad.

This mistrust has spoiled the so-called developed countries in social, economic and psychological terms. Just turn the pages of the history and compare judiciously who is better-we- people or our forefathers? Question yourself honestly whether you would be able to live your life like that and I am sure your answer will be in the negative. I am not advocating which time was better but my aim is just to make your thinking mature so that you should not spoil the life of your kids.

Everything and everyone is not bad

A successful person does not trust or mistrust blindly but he uses rationale to do so. You are a successful person and going to get more feathers in your cap. You may think how I am able to know about you. It is very simple. Once you have chosen this book from number of books lying on the book shelf, it denotes that you are a successful person. A person like you has to be inquisitive and mature otherwise success shall fall in wrong ends.

> **Trust and mistrust are relative terms. It shapes your personality and success and failure is the direct result of developing your mind accordingly.**

Trust and mistrust are relative terms. It shapes your personality and success and failure are the direct result of your mind. You must have heard the famous proverbs which read : "Birds of the same feather flock together" or as you sow, so shall you reap." You can't expect a mango fruit from a margosa tree. If you feel everyone is bad, you would find only bad people around you this, you must blame yourself, not any system or individual. I have encountered very few people who I cannot trust. But I trusted all others and they also had full faith in me.

Trust and mistrust are not just a state of mind and once you form an idea about anything or any person, it is very difficult to shed it. Our thinking shapes our personality and every thought is imbibed by our personality.

In order to win a war, we must start with a positive attitude and if something goes wrong, we should accept it as a natural cause. If we lose the war, we should have another start, with new zeal and initiative. When a person has to travel a long distance in life, he must have a positive attitude. One can't be hundred per cent right or wrong. We should concentrate on the right only to gain the maximum and achieve the result according to our plans.

Always be positive

Always be positive and feel that everything and everyone on this earth is good. In case something happens which you don't like, take it as an accident that can happen to anyone anytime. An accident would remain an accident only and it does not require any explanation. A positive thinker looks forward to doing again after learning a lesson. A negative thinker does not learn lessons from the accidents of the past, so he repeat mistakes.

No one is a born positive or negative thinker but it is his upbringing which shapes him accordingly. If you belong to a family where everyone disbelieves everyone else, it is certain that you shall imbibe this characteristic, as you would grow in an environment of mistrust. It will lower your self-esteem and make you seek favours from everyone.

An average person with average talent, ambition and education can outstrip the most brilliant genius in our society, provided that the person has clear, focused goals. The same is also true when that person has a positive attitude. In order to be successful, high-quality intelligence and brilliance are not required. Glance through the life stories of the successful people in and around you would get numerous examples of such people; all of them were not very intelligent. It is the determination for chasing the goal which is required to achieve it; and it is a result of positive thinking.

An average person with average talent, ambition and education can outstrip the most brilliant genius in our society, if that person has positive attitude.

You must repeat that you are a successful individual and then, see the difference in your personality. Whenever you repeat good sentences and thoughts you get charged with positive energy. It forces you to take positive actions only. When nothing moves according to your wish, you can think positively.

During a phase in my life, I also witnessed a time during my life when my brother who had been always obedient to me, had not been so cordial, my daughter disagreed to my decision for the first time and my son did not perform in the examination as per my expectation. The projects on which I was working, were to others. My Chairman was expecting some better result from me and I was unable to come up to his expectations. For the time being, I was busy sorting out all these. This crisis period went on for a week and I was not in a position to control the circumstances.

One night, my wife who, had been observing me for a week and knowing everything asked me, "What will happen if I die today?" It is the title of one of my books which happened to be one of the best sellers in the category of self-help books. For the time being I thought that a lady, who has always carried out the instructions given by me, may not be able to give me a soothing experience.

It is my habit to give the gist of any book in detail which I happen to read. Once I was discussing with her one of the books of Robin Sharma. She suddenly asked me, "Have you ever thought why Robin did not have to mention anything about his wife in any of his books?" Robin has discussed about everything but has mentioned nothing about his wife. In order to prove my superiority, I told her that it does not make a difference. However, this question got suppressed somewhere in my subconscious mind.

On that night, she told me if a writer like Robin can forget to mention an important link of his life in his best-sellers, irrespective of the reason, why can't I forget everything and everyone and live a life which is meant for one only. She explained that my brothers are leading their independent life and my kids also have completed their education, so we must leave them to live their own life. She further added that when we got married I was a simple teacher and whatever I am today is a matter of pride for anyone.

Satisfy yourself with what you have

You feel that you know everything and you can handle all the situations but it does not always happen in the way you calculate. We always forget to realize that satisfaction in life is a relative word and one may not be able to get the same till one desire to get the same. Remember the famous proverb which read, "The other side of the grass is always greener." The grass is greener till you go there and actually witness the same. As soon as you will reach there, you will find out the reality. It is not that it happens with all. The difference is someone realizes it early and someone takes a lot of time to realize it.

On the occasion of Holi (the festival of colours), a sale was declared to sell grooms on the biggest departmental store in the city. Anyone who will purchase a groom will get a discount of eighty per cent and a three bedroom flat as bonus in the most posh colony of the city. The store had six floors and the condition was that once a lady crossed a floor, she would not be allowed to come back to that floor and she would get only one chance to purchase. From the top floor, there was a way out of the building.

A lady went to the departmental store to get her right groom. She went to the first floor and saw a board which read, "These grooms are in jobs". After reading the board, the lady thought that on this floor, the grooms were better than her present boy friend but she tried to look at the next floor in search of someone better. She went to the second floor and there it read, "These guys have jobs and they love their kids too." The lady liked the deal but thought of seeing the other floors too. She went to the third floor and there it was written, "These guys have jobs, love their kids and look handsome." The lady decided to see the fourth floor too. It was written on the entrance of the floor, "These guys have jobs, love their kids, look handsome and help their wife in household tasks also." The lady became very happy. But she wanted to get a better deal, so she wanted to see the fifth floor also. She went there and it read, "These guys have jobs, love there kids, look handsome, help in household tasks and listen faithfully to their spouse." These qualities boosted the morale of the lady and she decided to see the grooms at the sixth floor also.

She went to the sixth floor and its notice board read, "You are customer number 123456789. On this floor, there is no guy and it proves that it is very difficult to satisfy you. Thank you for coming to this shopping mall and we shall see you again at some other time."

We must remember that without taking the first step, we can't reach the top of the ladder. This first step may not be a quality step but it is essential to go further. We go on improving with our every step till we get the required quality. Even after that we can't claim that further improvement is not possible. You must have observed the continuous improvement in the field of telecommunication. Starting from Bell's communication to "I Phone a journey of nearly three years and continuous Kaizen resulted in the best devise and technologies. But new things would arrive in future.

Success is a continuous process

Success is a mantra which you have to go on reciting. The recitation must be from the core of your heart; it will remind you to go further to do something better than others. Once you are accustomed of doing and getting better, congratulate yourself for being successful. Here, you have to remember not to stop but to move further with greater speed and stamina. Remember, your continuous speed in proportion to your worth will give you the result if you have faith in yourself.

> **Don't indulge in fighting or teaching lessons to others, else the enemy will come to know about your worth.**

In this course of action, don't indulge in fighting or teaching lessons to others else the enemy will come to know about your worth. You have been blessed with a unique potential for your own utilization and not to boast of the same. Boasting of your potential will not give you any result and a person like you should not do any piece of work which does not have any piece of sense of accomplishment or mental satisfaction.

There is nothing in this world which does not have any utility. The only thing is that sometimes, we are unable to know exactly the productivity of a person, place or thing due to our very conservative thinking. An individual, who understands the formula of nature gets the crown. Success is like a mathematical problem. In a class, all students are taught by the same teacher having the same book for the same time but the capability of solving a sum varies drastically from one student to another. One thing is also amazing, if you notice. You will also be amazed to know that given enough time most of the students will be able to solve the problem.

The problems in life fall in the same category. Those, who solve them fast, get an edge over others and enjoy the maximum benefit. It is the consistency and competencies of individuals which play vital roles. This difference, between quick-solving and delayed solving, differentiates you from the rest of the population. It is the reality of life which one must understand.

In life, it is not always the person having a high IQ who wins the race but the individual, who has consistency in his work, becomes the winner. Losers are envious of him not because he became a winner but because he won due to some partiality. You will be amazed to analyze that most of the natural and scientific postulates are true life.

A man was driving his car while it was raining heavily. Suddenly his left rear tyre got punctured and he had to stop. He opened the rear wheel. He unscrewed all the four screws but suddenly, all the four screws slipped out of his hand and went into the drain which was overflowing due to heavy rain. He was doing all this in front of a mental asylum and his action was under the constant watch of a patient of that asylum. The patient came near him and told him to take out one screw each from the other three wheels to start the journey. The man was surprised to learn why he was in the mental asylum whereas he was a genious. The patient replied that his suggestion was an issue demanding common sense and nothing more.

Success is not sudden

Success is never sudden unless you win a lottery and become a company owner overnight. Gradual success prepares you gradually to digest the effects. Hence, you will be mentally and physically ready to accept the success which is essential to lead a normal and balanced life.

An old man, nearly ninety years of age, got the confirmation of winning a lottery of 50 crore rupees and everyone was worried, as he was a critical heart patient wanted to shock him by breaking this news to him. At last, they decided to consult his physician who had been looking after him for a long time. The old man's kin wanted him to share this news with the old man so that in case anything happen the doctor would be able to take care.

The doctor visited the man next morning and told the old man that he was doing well and wanted to have a cup of tea with him in the lawn. Over a cup of tea, the doctor asked the old man what would he do in case he won a lottery of 50 crores. Immediate was the reply that he would offer 25 crores to his doctor who had saved him twice from the heart attack. Shockingly, the doctor collapsed immediately upon nearing this news.

Sudden success cannot be digested as it gives you pleasure which is beyond your control. Preparing to accept success is very important and it should not be allowed to be shown in physical terms or through our body language.

In life, you have to start from somewhere to reach somewhere. This somewhere is your goal which may be as small as getting one-time meal and bigger like being an individual who would `provide meals to thousands daily. But in order to achieve the second goal, you must achieve the first one. If you don't take stand on anything, everything will slip from your hand. Your first stand will decide your future.

If you don't take stand on anything, everything will slip from your hand.

Man, by nature, is very choosy and he looses most of the chances due to this nature. Being choosy is not bad but it is also not advisable to miss the first step in this course of action, otherwise one will have no other option but repent. It is not that no one knows it but very few of us take it wisely. You must have noticed a number of individuals who will go on blaming the whole world that would have proved their worth, they had got a chance.

You have to work consistently and in a planned manner to achieve failure your goals. These processes take time. Do not be frustrated due to failures; they are part of everyone's life. You must keep on working hard, despite all odds. Finally, success would be achieved in your area of operation. It would be hard-earned success.

Every problem has a solution

We are being forced to listen from our childhood that life is not a bed of roses and it requires something extra to lead a peaceful and happy life. This proverb always interfered with my thought process. I am of the opinion– why one should want a red-carpet treatment for leading his life at someone else's cost and labour. Anything, which is received without labour, does not give the satisfaction of achievement and after some time, it ceases to give you any happiness, whereas a small achievement after a tireless efforts gives you great satisfaction.

The achievement motive of an individual differs drastically and it gets imbibed in the individual's characters due to his belief in himself. As you have belief in yourself, you will have the killer instinct to achieve the thing you desire. Problems are part and parcel of life and one should not get stressed while facing them. The more problems you face in life the faster would be your decision making capacity. The problems actually sharpen your decision making capacity and you get a chance of feeling better than the person who has no problems to solve.

One must understand that there is no lock without a key and there will not be any problem without a solution. If you want to achieve something better than others, be fearless and face today's problem only and forget to blame anyone for the problems you are encountering. However, you should thank the individual who is making you capable of solving these riddles of life and giving you a chance to be recognized.

There is no lock without a key and there will not be any problem without a solution.

Man believes that a problem is the product of someone near and dear to him who wants to see him in trouble, irrespective of his achievements. It happens, as most of us have developed negative thinking over a span of time and can't believe that something good can happen to us. Such negative feelings had got entrenched inside us that we forget to accept the usefulness of encountering problems in our daily life.

Believe it or not, you will not get any successful individual on this earth who has someone else to solve his problems, irrespective, of his mental make up. It is also true that once you are successful in your area of operation, you may employ a number of persons to take care of your problems. It is not that by hiring other individuals, you would proceed to take rest but be sure that you are going to be involved in solving bigger problems of life and business. It is the way of life of a successful individual. Actually, success is the direct outcome of your problem-solving aptitude.

In sum, you must concentrate on achieving more important and pious goals in life. You should allocate small tasks and goals to people under you. Develop your problem-solving ability by taking a tongh challenge.

This should not be very tough in the beginning. Solve this problem and enhance the level of difficulty in the next assignment. That way, you would develop gradually yet surely. Do not try to reach the top of the ladder by leaping upto the highest wrung of the ladder. No one could succeed that way. Every riddle can be solved. The only thing is that time, efforts and resources, besides your brain, are need to tackle the riddle in a most efficient manner.

•

Chapter 4

Create Your Own World

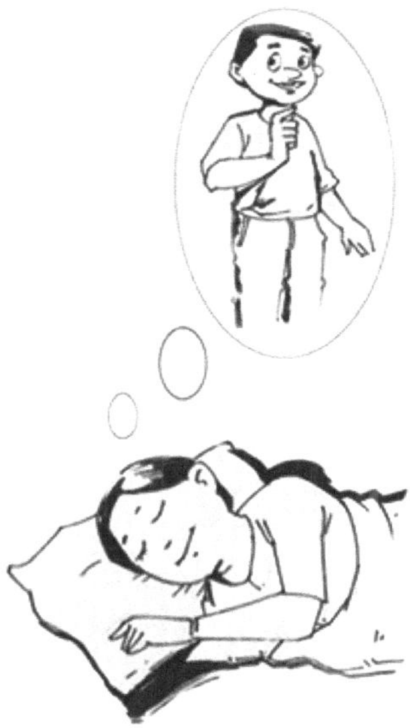

Every living being on this earth has got the capacity to do and create the things according to his own choice, irrespective of the situations he faces. The differences among individuals are nothing else but the way of getting things done. Dreams are not what we see when we are asleep. Rather, a real dream does not allow us to sleep.

Dream is not what we see when we are asleep.Rather, a real dream does not allow us to sleep.

Once, we have decided to achieve something then all our actions are directed towards achieving that end. We feel energized to achieve the same. The killer instinct behind this is the motivating force. The dream which we see while we are awake shapes our future and helps in creating our own world.

The vision of life of any individual depends upon his upbringing and surroundings. You must have noticed that in this world, you get what exactly you want but you may not get what you had desired for. The difference between 'need' and 'desire' is the intensity to which we miss that thing in our life. One may miss a day's meal where–another individual may miss a tour of space in a newly designed spacecraft by the ISRO. To miss something in life is directly proportional to the things which we possess. We can't miss something which we already have and also not the similar things what we possess.

Every successful individual on this earth has created a world for himself within the existing one where everyone is living. The shape and size of an individual's world will decide his destiny. The bigger the dream, the bigger would be this creation, as one has to accommodate so many things. The decision of creating something for our own satisfaction is in itself a big thinking which accelerates other types of thinking into action.

Success in itself is not something which one can celebrate but its effect makes an individual happier or ecstatic. It creates a sense of upgrading in the individual who yearns for it. You should not have seen a person who never tries to be better than what he is but the achievement of betterment depends upon his belief in himself. The better the belief of an individual in himself, the better would be the task accomplished by him.

Most of us have a habit of asking for a lighter load but very few of us ask the Almighty for a stronger back. We forget that trusting in God won't make the mountain smaller but trust would certainly make the climb easier. The thinking of every individual differs drastically and the result is directly proportional to this belief and thinking only. The positive thinking makes us happy and rewarding all the time whereas the opposite will be the outcome with the negative thinking.

> **Trusting in God won't make the mountain smaller but trust would certainly make the climb easier.**

The world will be same for everyone whether you are a gainer or a looser. The person, who gets something positive in this world, faces the same friction as the one who looses something here.

Your achievement in this world is the result of your thinking and belief in you only and not in someone else. Your competitor may be more intelligent and powerful than you but he may not be as fast as you in making an event to happen. A good swimmer is not an individual who knows all the tricks but is the one who makes an immediate decision of positively reacting to the swimming competition.

Have faith in yourself

A farmer in America used to get first prize every year. He had been winning the first prize for the past ten years for his best maize product. A TV channel reporter tried to find out the details for making breaking news for his channel. He approached the farmer and the farmer asked him to stay with him when the harvest season approached. The TV reporter stayed there and to his surprise, he saw one morning that the farmer took out the maize seed stored in his house and started distributing the same to his neighbours so that they could also sow the same seed along with him. The reporter was surprised. Seeing the face of the reporter, the farmer understood his query. So, he called all his farmer friends for a discussion with the reporter. He introduced everyone and said, "They are my neighbour friends and our area of operation is the same. Everyone has some special quality, as I know how to spot good seed. In the same way my closest neighbour understands to predict the weather condition. Another one is an expert in managing the field and so on. Hence, every one of us is an expert in any one of the areas of maize production."

The farmer further added, "we all share our experience and materials and that is why we are successful in getting the prize. When I get any award, I share that with my colleagues and become happy. That is why no one is jealous of anyone. This team spirit shocked the reporter, as this policy was contrary to his profession. In the media, everyone tried to pull the leg of others to be the first one in the fray.

You can be a winner by defeating everyone who is with you in the race and prove yourself that you are the only individual who has the worth. A weak person can never have such thinking, as he will always be afraid of his own status. It helps in two ways. First you get the satisfaction of helping everyone around you. Second, live in a society of winners. It can only happen once you are confident of your worth, knowing honestly what you are.

This can only happen when you get the feeling that this world has enough for everyone to fulfill their need but not enough to fulfill their greed. The 'need' and 'greed' concepts help you to know yourself better, as the definitions of need and greed will be different for different individuals. Sometimes, they would be different for same individual irrespective of the change of time and place. An individual who has evaluated his worth will be more confident than the one having more worth but not estimated the same.

You may recall the story from the famous epic, Ramayana in which everyone was sitting by the side of the sea and discussing how to cross the sea and go to Sri Lanka. Everybody was evaluated but no one was coming close to the target. Hanuman was not participating but when someone reminded him of his worth, he immediately presented himself as a choice to complete the assigned task. He came to know his worth after being reminded by someone.

In this world you can get everything, provided you must pursue that earnestly. Once you pursue something, your worth will force you to fill the gap by achieving the same. The deeper you will go pursuing, deeper would your worth expects you to put action to accomplish the goal. It will be your action will determine the time of achievement.

Contentment and Saving for Future

The biggest second recession of this century till date made everyone believe that Indian culture is the best which forces a family to save for its future. The greatest sufferer this recession is the USA where people spent more than what they earned. They took loan from banks and financial institutions thinking that the time will never change. Being the most civilized country on this earth that shows the best path to most of the developing countries. But Uncle Sam's blunder is very difficult to accept and the result was total economic fiasco for this economic super-power.

Weeping over spilt milk is foolishness, as you can't rewind that action. The day you start with a feeling of happiness with what you have, you would celebrate every day, as you would have known the secret of a successful life. Thinking about the things we don't have and making life miserable would take us nowhere.

A fisherman was disturbed over a family matter, so he left his house to go to the river bed for fishing. It was very dark, as the sun was behind clouds. In order to kill his time he started walking along the river bank. Suddenly, he hit a bag having shining stones in it. In order to kill his time, he started throwing stones one by one in the river. When he was about to throw the last piece of stone, the Sun appeared in the sky and he was amazed to see the shining stone in his hand. He gazed at the stone and was surprised to note that it was a piece of precious diamond!

He started weeping bitterly and was unable to believe that he threw so many diamonds in the river. In the mean time, a saint approached him and came to know the reason of his sorrow.

He said, "My dear son, don't weep. You should be happy. Still, you are fortunate. It is your luck that you kept holding in the last piece of diamond, otherwise it would have also gone into the river. Only this diamond would be able to change your whole life." He further added, "The thing which has slipped from your hand has got no value for you whereas you must celebrate for what you have."

It is your thinking which brings everything to you, irrespective of what your worth is. Sometimes, you are amazed to see something happening exactly in the way you wished, irrespective of all odds. It is nothing but the indirect perspective of your productive thinking which delivers the result even when you are not sure of the result.

Conditions may be favourable or unfavourable but your thinking process must always be under your control. You think what you miss or try to achieve. In both the cases, you propel your mind to act in the direction of your thinking and respond accordingly. Sometimes, we get confused due to our needs and desires and our mind is unable to comprehend our actions. In order to get a quicker and far-reaching response, we must be clear what actually we need and what actually we desire.

Only think about what you miss or try to achieve.

A happy person would radiate positive energy in the environment. He would be able to show his happiness to a number of individuals around him. So, would make his own life as well as the life of others happy and comfortable. Thus good and positive thinking can make our mind open for accepting new ideas. It is ready for ideas as the process is fast and according to the need of the individual.

To be happy or not, is solely an individual's decision and he only has control over this. It is also learnable behaviour and by constant practice one can learn to be and to make someone happy. When you keep yourself under your control, no body can make you unhappy, irrespective of the situation you may be facing. The essence of our great epic, Mahabharata, lies in this thought. It has been clearly mentioned in that epic that you need not to worry for the result of any action, as the action is under your influence and control but not the result.

A process may differ from action to action but for a particular individual, the processes also bear some similarity and it may influence your action. It is always advised that we must be free from any ailment before starting any piece of work to avoid negative thinking and actions. Sometimes, we are so influenced by a particular condition or individual that we can't think or except what that condition or individual force us to do.

In order to be successful in your group, you must inculcate the habit of making yourself happy, irrespective of the situations. You must indulge in positive thinking and you shall get positive results. Through regular practice, you would be able to get the result as per your desire.

Do what you feel is right

I have worked with many organizations. Once, I came across an individual who was a young boy of twenty-six and had started a school with an investment of nearly eight hundred lakhs Rupees. Since his father was in real estate business and he had completed his management degree, he thought that education was the best business during these days of recession. Someone introduced him to me and he fixed up an appointment with me. He came to my residence at the appointed time and while discussing the project, he was very sure that money can purchase anything. He was not wrong, as he had seen this only in his formative years of his life as well as business.

After discussion, when he came to know my consultancy fee, he was surprised. It was clear from his gesture that he was unable to digest the amount which was asked for getting something done in his school within a span of nearly a month. He tried to convince me that the amount which I was charging was too much and that he knew a number of people who were about to join this new business and that he could recommend my name to them. I am not against bargaining in business but I am really against the way people talk while discussing something with an educationist. There is a general feeling that educationists do not deserve a nice price for the services rendered by them. I did not tell anything to him but I was unable to control my habit of teaching the right thing to everyone whoever comes in my contact. I told him a story. It goes as follows:

Picasso, the famous painter, was taking rest after a brisk walk. In the meantime, a lady, who was one of her admirers, approached him and wanted her portrait made. Picasso wanted to refuse but seeing her admiration towards him he did the work in a short interval of time. Later, he asked the lady to pay him a sum of 1000 Dollars.

It was the time for the lady to be astonished, as Picasso took only five minutes to draw the portrait. When he observed that the lady was hesitating to pay such a huge amount after working for so less time, Picasso said to her, "Madam, for the five minutes of labour, the fee is only 5 Dollars but the rest of the amount is for the experience of getting the work finished within five minutes."

The lady was fully convinced and sent a cheque of 1000 Dollars to Picasso the next day.

There was no doubt that the boy was brilliant, so he understood the message at once and we did four projects together. He reminds me that I charge heavily. Although he does it to cut a joke but one can assume that this thinking is somewhere in his subconscious mind. As a teacher, I always try to make him understand that education is the hub of all societal changes and as a business, it is above any recession, whether it is of the 2008 – 2009 or of the 1929- 1930 period.

In our society, if you are governed by what people say and think about yourself, you are doomed. That is because none of these people are really concerned about you a point of discussion to kill their time they want to make. Pushing someone to fall and laugh later is a cruel act and from any viewpoint, this act cannot be termed as a humane gesture.

Such personalities are omnipresent and one must be careful of such people and should think and do what one feel is correct, justified and according to the norm of society. You should never undertake any work just to please someone, else you would get negative pleasure from that action. You should always be ready to justify your action, not to prove someone else that you are right but to convince yourself that you are right and just.

You will encounter so many individuals who would try to shake your belief in yourself, not to gain anything from you but to make you like them. They are the unsuccessful lot on this earth, blaming everyone for their failure, except themselves just to gain sympathy. They will never tolerate any other individual becoming successful and to rule them for their utter failure which was due to their inefficiency and lethargy.

Never shake anyone's faith

The basic difference between winners and losers is the way of handling their commitement. The winners are never cheats; and a cheat can never be a winner. One day, one of my friends asked, "If I break your faith one day, what will happen?" My answer was quick, "To have faith is my decision, my right and to prove me right is your decision." Faith is a universal action which requires a good commitment about one's own self as well.

One day, one of my friends asked "If I break your faith one day, what will happen?" My answer was quick, "To have faith is my decision, my right and to prove me right or wrong is your decision."

In your life, you would find many individuals who are not very particular about keeping faith and promise. They are of the view that only individuals having weak personality have faith to cover their incompetence. But in reality, it is just the opposite; faith and promises can only be kept by individuals who have strong and straightforward personality. The brave can only pardon anyone and the reverse of it is not seen under a normal situation.

Make yourself known as a person who never tries to ditch anyone at any cost. You don't require such cheap tactics to be better than others. Let people know that you practise your own ethics and care for your ethical values. There may be a time that you have to loose something because of your ethical values but in the long run, you will be a winner in your area of operation.

People feel that while working for someone else, they may not be able to practise their values but it is not true. Let your employer clearly know that you have sold your time to him, not your self-respect. He is free to get anything done within the required time limit but you may not be able to do any unethical practice irrespective of the tact that you may get a lucrative thing in return. It is better to say goodbye than to buckle under to such pressure which would keep you remorseful till you are alive and force you to have artificial happiness on your face.

A quick view around you will give you several examples in this context. You must be very clear in your thinking that if you don't get anything due to your hard labour, it is sure that you would not be able to get the same through your unethical source as well. There may be a time that you may not be able to get return of your hard labour. Adequate task(s) it your destiny and go on doing the same without loosing your faith and passion in yourself. Be sure that no one can stop you from getting the result. If you are getting a mediocre result, don't get perturbed; the future is yours which is sure to compensate you.

Until and unless you keep the promise made by you to yourself and learn to honour the same, you can't be honoured by others. A person, who is not honest to himself, can, in no way, be honest to others. The biggest and the most sensible promise is to make yourself happy and feel that you are as important as others. Most of us are very nice to others but not to self or family members.

The person who is not honest to himself, can, in no way be honest to others.

The reason behind it is that most of us carry a split personality which is different for us and others. We forget that while telling lies, we have to remember the lie, otherwise we may tell some other lie which may not be in tune with the previous one.

The honesty towards your values gives uniqueness to your character. A unique character is a whole life in itself and people are always eager to know the details of your character. You have to adopt a set of good values and stick to the same. By practicing such characteristics, you are making yourself reliable in the eyes of people; and that would transpile without any investment. Here, the investment is in the form of hidden cost which may include your straight solution to any problem directly related to your value system. Out of thousands and thousands of people on this earth, only few live for ever and you are going to be one amongst in case you stick to your value system without fail.

Master your attitude

You are an individual who is born independent and wants to remain independent. It can happen when you develop an attitude of gratitude and give thanks for everything that happens to you. Every step you take should be a step toward for achieving something bigger and better than your current level of achievement. People fall into two categories. One group believes that in this world, everyone should behave with them in a nice way as they are nice person.

The other group comprises individuals who feel that every bad thing would happen to all others in this world but never to them. They also believe that once they have not done anything wrong to someone; nothing wrong can happen to them. This thinking is like the person who is a good driver and expects that no one will dash him as he is the best driver.

The attitude of a person determines his altitude.

The attitude of a person determines his altitude. Edmund Hilary climbed Mount Everest only because he had an attitude of doing something special which none else had done till date. It was not America was not on the earth till Columbus discovered. It was there on the earth but it was not there on the map of the world. The attitude of Columbus to discover something special brought America in front of the world. It was not an ordinary attitude but it was a determined attitude which did not allow Columbus to take rest till he got his dream fulfilled of America.

Everyone has this attitude but it is the killer instinct which makes someone special. Such people don't take rest till they achieve the desired level of perfection. This desired level of perfection varies from individual to individual; and time also plays crucial role in it. You will witness a number of individuals who start any work with all fanfare but end abruptly, as they can't concentrate on the work for a longer span of time. It is not that they will not be able to achieve the set goal but their attention level is so low that, they would switch over to some other piece of work. They think that the new target will be easy to achieve but in reality, it is not so.

The attitude of such individuals is versatile and t hey, irrespective of their creative attitude, fail to achieve what is fit to them. Such individuals fail to understand that success begets success and achieving something less important is not going to stop you to achieve a bigger target in the queue. Once you achieve something, it forces you to move further with greater speed and pointed actions.

It is not that you and your viewpoint would easily be accepted by everyone. Rather, you must remember that Bill Gates and Dhirubhai Ambani became a laughing stock because of their ideas as their ideas were far ahead of their times. The general public were unable to digest their new view or business ideas. It always happens and those, who come up with their (new) idea, become a source of ridicule for everyone.

Your attitude about yourself as well as about your thinking shapes your future. You must be very fair about your thinking and any doubt arising in your mind should be clarified at the earliest to give a scope for further enquiry generation. This enquiry generation acts as fresh air. People may take you as a moody person due to your stubborn attitude but you have to generate courage to nullify the same. One has to be alone on the path of success, as a crowded path would lead one to a known destination only. Note that a known destination may not be the destination of success for you.

Those individuals, who have been successful, are those who wanted to be unique they had changed their attitude to suit their success story. It is not that you should not be considerate towards others views but it has to be up to the extent of retaining your individualistic style of thinking. You should be able to do some special tasks without disturbing anyone.

Don't be afraid of criticism

A person without any criticism is a person who has not been noticed and does not have any ability. We criticize those people who are different from others and have something unique that makes them special. It is not that such individuals are always productive and give something to society but in most of the cases, their thinking is far ahead of the thinking of ordinary people. They believe in themselves and feel comfortable in the company of their critics.

Jal and Imran were two actors. They were harshly criticized by the Press. Jal was so angry and upset that he immediately wrote a harsh letter defending himself and flaying the critics in a very harsh tone. The relationship a between these two men was so strained that it was difficult to carry it forward.

Imran slept over the matter. One day the sting was less severe. Then, he wrote to his critic, thanking him for pointing out certain weaknesses in his performance and assuring him that his criticism was welcome. The kind reply touched the critic and the two became lasting friends.

Criticism can often be very constructive and helpful. However, praise is mere flattering and does not teach us much.

Remember the contributions of all discoverers and you will find one thing in common among all of them. They were never accepted in society and in most of the cases, their invention had become popular after death. Not only this, most of the top corporate houses became a name to reckon with in their second or third generations. In the first generation the ideas which they imbibed were in their infancy and seemed to be like fairy tales to most people. They started with their thinking with firm determination and made it a question of their survival. Idea in itself has no life but it is the determination of an individual which gives it life.

Idea in itself has no life but it is the determination of an individual which gives it life.

During the summer holidays of 2001, when I was sitting in my office finishing and giving shape to my new agenda, I received a visiting card through my PA. The lady was waiting at the reception to meet me. She had been sent by one of the professors from the Indian Institute of Management, Ahmedabad. The professor was my course director for a short term programme on Strategic Leadership Management. This programme had been organized by the Central Board of Secondary Education (CBSE) for its selected principals who were in the team for inspection of new schools to be affiliated to CBSE.

I called the lady actually, she was a young girl accompanied by her friend. They told me that they had completed their B. Tech. from IIT Kanpur and immediately got seats in the IIM through CAT. Their rank in both IIT and CAT was within the first ten and they belonged to a business family of Surat. I was amazed to learn that they wanted to know the basic details for starting a school. On further discussion, I came to know that they had got nice placement with high salary brackets in the finance sector abroad. However, they decided to go ahead with their venture without any support of their family which they were not getting due to their unique project.

The idea of opening a school came to their mind while doing their project on the education sector as a requirement of the project to be done during the MBA programme. They were of the opinion that the crisis in the field of education (mainly school education) is the result of a historical neglect of the education by industry and its failure to provide leadership to the former. Now that education itself is being seen as a social obligation and industry needs diversified talent, it is the time for industry to step in to take more active role in our school education system.

They were of the opinion that there is confusion about the status of education whether it is a charity or a business. The normal investment route is shut for education and it is dependent by and large on the largesse of trusts or personal funding of the promoter groups. Its running expenses are completely self-financed, with bank funding limited to building construction. This dissuades out professionals and industries from entering the field of education.

The only thing about which they were sure was their success and they got by getting their school established in six years as one of the best managed academic institutions at Gandhinagar in Ahmedabad. The reverse might have been true by joining any finance firm and getting salary in Dollars but they made themselves ready to listen to criticism and used it to propel them towards success.

Be part of the solution

You encounter so many people on a daily basis who are of the opinion that they are born problem-solvers and that their decision-making capacity is superb. They also have a feeling that people should approach them for any of their problems starting from the repair of a mobile phone to admission of their kids to particular stream. If you happen to look into the family life of these people, you will be amazed to note that they are fiascos at their home front and they feel that they are doing a lot to society.

Problems would be there, irrespective of the time and circumstances. Problems sharpen our decision making capacity and add salt to our life for a better and changed taste of living. They are our true friends in the sense that they make us realize about our capacity and capabilities. A life without problems is a recipe without any taste.

In our daily life, we come across another set of people who have a habit of creating problems for others and try to solve the same to prove their supremacy over others. They are smart people and want to be branded like the same. Their marketing goes on flourishing on a daily basis and even people having higher IQ regard them better than themselves. The only thing which they forget is that we can't solve a problem in a way we generate it. This is the very basis of problem-solving attitude.

We can't solve a problem in a way we generated it.

There is no problem in helping to remove the frustration of someone but there is a problem when you tell others that you can solve all riddles, answer all questions or help one and all. These are utopian statements and ought not be given. A person, who is striving for success, refrains himself from such thinking.

If you want to run fast and also, to be ahead of others, you should certainly think of being superior than the individuals who are with you in this race. However, you should never think yourself as the best, or the one who does not require any correction at any stage. Time changes at its own speed and so should you. That is possible only when you are part of a solution and not a problem at any stage of your life.

The individuals who have got their names inscribed their names in the annals of history are those who have always seen the problem for getting a solution from the data available. Babar, the founder of Mughal empire in India, came as a robber on the invitation of Ibrahim Lodi who wanted to teach a lesson to his enemies. Babar immediately judged the attitude of Indian kings and decided to settle in India by defeating Ibrahim Lodi only.

The decision radiates through any problem; you have to watch this radiation and catch hold of it at the right time. The solution of a problem may or may not be beneficial immediately but its evaluation would give you a correct notion of its implication in future. We should not see a problem with a convergent thinking attitude but we must scrutinize it for getting a permanent solution. Basically, we should always concentrate on the disease than the symptom which may not give true indications.

The failure in solving any problem certainly does not testify your caliber, as you may not have diagnosed the problem in a correct way. It should not lower your self-esteem. That is because by changing the prospective of the situation you may be able to get a solution of the same. It requires a continuous and fair stock taking of the situation which can help in solving the problem. Keeping eyes and mind open for suggestions solves most of your problems which you encounter.

A successful individual is always in need of new ideas which are possible when he allow everyone to speak up to give a suggestion. Getting suggestions increases his chance of getting a better and most acceptable solution. If he has a view no one can think better than him, then his progress stops. People who have been successful in this world, were alone but they had never discarded the suggestions put forth by others. Your share of thinking is always with you but, in addition, if you get the views and suggestions of others, what is the harm in it?

Review progress daily

You might have witnessed that when you get a thing which you have desired, you think of getting a better item than what you have obtained. It is not that you are a unique thinker; rather it happens with all of us. For self progress and for the progress of society, such thinking is appreciated to some extent. It suggests that the road to success is always under construction.

The road to success is always under construction.

After reaching one coveted destination, we are relaxed for a while. However, we start thinking of pushing ahead. Human beings are target oriented and want to be different from the rest. After reaching a particular place, when he notices that others are approaching the same spot, a person forgets the troubles he had encountered during the last journey. He starts for a new destination. It goes on till he can undertake the journey. It is a peculiar psychology of man. He never gets satisfied with what he has and he always thinks of what he can have.

It's your thinking which makes you special. You are like all other individuals. Most people will never notice you in case you are a routine thinker, as there are many routine thinkers here and there. You have to be a day-dreamer to get noticed. Once you are noticed, people around you seem to get something special from you and this recognition of people generates extra energy inside you which propel you to get something extra from you.

Success has different connotations for people. It also has different hues at different times to same individual. It's the quest of success which makes you successful. Sometimes you know and work on the dotted line and sometimes, you go on doing unknowingly and get something special and this forces you to go in the direction of getting more and more. It is your never ending appetite which brings name and fame for you. People come and go in this world but successful persons stay in this world for ever. The Wright Brothers became immortal. It is not that they had invented Sukoi the fastest running fighter jet. They became legends because they had given a ground on which sukho has developed. If someone modifies your ideas after you get a result, you will always be there.

We think, start and desert in the middle most of the ideas which are really special. Chasing an idea and bringing it to take a shape are two very difficult task. Those, who do so, get branded as successful individuals. Time is important in all these actions but the most important thing is commitment. You may start a race but to be in the race and reaching the finishing point requires efforts and commitment. Sadly, very few of us have the will to make efforts and the commitment towards the goal.

A handsome gentleman went to a bank and wanted a loan of Rs.20,000/-. He was escorted to the manager of the bank. The manager enquired, "Do you have anything to keep with the bank as a security?"

The man answered, "Yes, I have this Mercedes car to keep as security." After checking all the documents and after being satisfied, the manager gave him Rs. 20,000 as loan and kept the vehicle as security.

The man returned after a year, went directly to the bank manager and made the full payment of the loan with interest. Out of curiosity, the manager asked the man, "From the tag tied with your bag it is clear that you are coming from the USA. Still you wanted a loan of only Rs.20,000/-."

The man replied, "I was alone. Who else could take care of my dearest vehicle so nicely in such a small amount for a year".

Your achievement level is decided by the way you think and perceive the situation. Everyone has the capacity but winners work on their ideas and the looser loose else a the idea to make someone else a winner. Persistent chasing of the idea makes you a winner and you get branded as a successful individual. You understand yourself, decide that you will do something better than others, swing into action without loosing any time and achieve the result. You will always get what you wanted but you have to make dedicated efforts, irrespective of your capacity and capability. A slight change in your thinking shall turn you to be a winner.

Treat past as history

India has a population of more than a million but still, we are branded as a nation having low potential. That is a reality, irrespective of the fact that we have been gifted with all natural resources and have the largest human resource. The root cause of this debacle is our thinking process which has been wrongly designed since our childhood. We were told, from the very beginning, to be satisfied with what we had and to look below the line in case we want to be happy. The world seems to one a place where everyone is cheated and one has to be careful at every stage.

> **Continuous efforts, not strength or intelligence, are the key to unlock our potential.**

Note that continuous efforts, not strength or intelligence, are the key for unlocking our potential.

In Shri Bhagwad Gita, Sri Krishna has always stressed on the efforts. He makes Arjuna understand that the only thing which is his contribution is his efforts and the result generated is directly proportional to the efforts which he would put in. Effort is the basic factor which carves the path of success for you. There is a great difference between strength and effort. A person may be stronger than others but lacking in efforts; this would make him an ordinary individual. The individuals, who have been successful on this earth, were not stronger and more intelligent than others. However, they put their continuous efforts to get what they dreamed.

Chasing the goal is more important than setting a goal. We are so suspicious towards everyone and every situation that we can never perceive something good happening to us. So, we must analyse people and situations from a positive angle and see how they can be fruthful to you or others.

You must remember that success requires moderate intelligence only and it is not as important as effort. Take a look at the personalities who have been successful in this world. Interestingly, most of them were even less intelligent than a normal individual but due to their continuous efforts in their desired direction they got results.

They also faced failures. They also received brickbats from the public. They also got the setbacks. But they never cared and at last people accepted them as winners and successful individuals. After they delivered the result, everyone started thinking that they would also have delivered the same as they were more intelligent than them. But they ignored the basic thing that they themselves lacked continuous efforts which the successful individuals did without fail.

Efforts are never wasted and we have to keep this crucial fact in mind. It is important to do the efforts in the right direction. A right direction is the one in which you have your goal. This may or may not be right for others but may be perfectly right for you. You should never have a doubt about your goal once you have decided to pursue it. Minor deviation may give better result but major deviation from your goal would lead you nowhere. Carrying burden in this form of a goal would waste your energy and efforts. Your success would always reward you but it is not restricted to you only. Society should be benefited from what you achieve.

It is not the time to devote any more energy but to start your efforts in the direction of your thinking and be sure that something beyond sky is your limit. Persistent effort shall never be wasted and you shall get the result. The basic recipe of success varies from individual to individual but the basic characteristics of successful people can be identified with ease. You may or may not have those characteristics but if you have stamina to do efforts, you shall be successful.

Be committed towards your action

Your action determines your forward movement. The momentum you gain in life to remain ahead of others is directly proportional to applied efforts. The applied efforts should be uniform and constant. The road to success is never uniform and so should be your speed.

The action and reaction part of life shapes your achievement level. You may like it or not but it is sure that you would have to determine your worth to gain something purposeful in life. Your determined action will be your worth and you must ensure that you are not fixing a target that is either higher or lower than your worth. Most of us start an action towards a goal without evaluating our worth. Actually, we set out by seeing someone else and having a notion that if someone else can do it why not we? This is not a bad idea but it would be beneficial if we evaluate our worth through comparison with that individual who has probably our role model in this case. You have to do your own SWOT analysis and compare it with your role model. After doing SWOT, you can be sure which qualities you have to imbibe and which weaknesses you have to shed off.

In a race, only one person will be the winner irrespective of that everyone in the race has the same ability. Nature always chooses the best. The best is always better than the rest. Sometimes, the best one loses the game since he is overconfident. The hare lost the race since he was overconfident, in spite of the fact that he was a far superb runner than the tortoise. The blunder the hare committed in this race was that he had agreed to run a race with an opponent who had nothing to lose if he was defeated. The second mistake he did was that once he had decided to run a race, he should have taken rest only after finishing the race.

In the race of life, the theory of probability holds true. The theory of probability states that you should take a chance only when the chance of being a winner and looser is not less than fifty per cent. This can only be decided after evaluating your worth which only you can do and none else. That is because you are your best SWOT analyzer. You may meet people who may motivate you. They may tell you that you can achieve anything and that most of the so called motivational books also propel you in this direction. Yes, you can but what is harm in evaluating your worth before taking any challenge and coming to know at a later stage that you were not having particular characteristics to be the winner? Your worth analysis gives you a correct assessment of your character and in case you are lacking something you should attain the same before you start action to achieve your goal.

You must remember that you have not taken birth to satisfy the needs of others but for yourself. What is good and bad for you, is for you to decide. Hence, logical evaluation is most important before you start any action. Once you become the master of this analysis and also conclude some fact, you start any work. You shall certainly succeed in that piece of work. All you need to do is do determined, preplanned actions for the sake of goal achievement. Cooks prepare all ingredients necessary for making a dish in advance and are ready to prepare any "dish" in least time. This saves their energy as well as helps them skip the duplication of labour.

The preparation for winning a battle is more important than fighting the battle. Once the battle starts, you may not get enough time to do the preparation. This preparation is on physical as well as mental front. Once you plan something, your brain analyzes everything and starts sending messages accordingly to keep you ready to face the relevant situation. The mental preparation for any action keeps you ahead of others and your brain is readily available for any damage control.

Always keep in mind that success requires only a medium amount of intelligence with some sprinkling of self-imagination and self-confidence. The individuals who have these qualities and are able to face failures are sure to be successful.

•

Chapter 5

Attitude: The Deciding Factor of Success

The Japanese have always loved to consume fresh fish. But the water close to Japan has not nurtured many fish for decades. So to feed the Japanese population, fishing boats got bigger, installed better equipment and went further on the high seas than ever. The farther the fishermen went, the longer it took them to bring back the fish. If the return trip took more time, the fish would not be fresh. In order to solve this problem, fishing companies installed freezers on their boats. They would catch the fish and freeze them at sea. Freezers allowed the boats to go further and

stay longer. However, the Japanese could taste the difference between fresh and frozen fish. They did not like the taste of frozen fish. The frozen fish brought a lower price for fish trawler owners and firms. So, fishing companies installed fish tanks aboard such boats. They would catch the fish and stuff them in the tanks, fin to fin. After a little smirching around, they were tired. They would become dull and lose their fresh-fish taste. The fishing industry faced an impending crisis! But today, they get fresh-tasting fish for the Japanese.

How did they manage? In order to keep the fish taste fresh, the Japanese fishing companies still put the fish in tanks but with a small shark in each one. The fish are challenged by the presence of the shark and hence, are constantly on the move. The challenge they face keeps them alive and fresh!

Have you realized that some of us are also living in a pond but most of the time we remain tired and dull? Basically in our lives, sharks are the new challenges to keep us active. If you are steadily conquering challenges, you are happy. Your challenges keep you energized. Don't create a success story to revel in it in a state of inertia. You have the resources, skills and abilities to make a difference. Put a shark in your tank and see how far you can really go!

It is the weakness of one's attitude which is directly responsible for bringing weakness in one's character. In turn, your personality gets shaped to the attitude developed and maintained by you. The shark put in the tank was not big enough to eat even a small fish but the weakness in the character the fish all the difference. It is made attitude which finally gets shaped permanently due to a perceived fear which in reality is not present. Most of us are one's victims of this phenomenon. Some of us analyse it and get out of it but most of us are fearful of even making an analysis of the same due to another perceived fear that the intensity of that phenomenon might increase.

The weakness of one's attitude brings weakness in character.

The attitude of the organizations to spend more than what they earned is the root cause of the recession that had occurred some years ago. The persons working in these organizations were so sure that nothing would go wrong and so, they did not develop any contingency plan to face such situations. They formed an easy-going attitude and comfortable-zone situations. When you work for yourself or for some organization you should only love your work and not the organization. Once you will love your work you will try to give the maximum to the organization by updating yourself and in turn it will make you comfortable to do something else in an adverse situation. But it does not happen as human being by its very nature always search for a comfortable zone and as soon as they achieve this comfort-zone status, they really becomes comfortable, even arrogant.

People, who have made history, were the ones who were always eager to get out of their comfort zone. As soon as they reached their comfort for zones, they immediately got out of it and move forward to search for another challenge. This process goes on for ever. In order to be successful, one must miss some thing (or luxurious) in life. A person, who has got settled in his permanent comfort zone, can never be a successful individual as he is satisfied with what he has.

Movement keeps us energetic and vibrant. Our movement is directly related to our attitude. A slow attitude results in slow movements. Energetic attitude, having an achievement motive, results in fast, steady and calculated movements. Movement keeps us mentally as well as physically fit. You must have noticed that those individuals, who work hard, are physically fit, they feel that a physical lethargy can cost them enormously.

Let us glance through the history of successful individuals. You will be amazed to note that all of them had positive attitude about themselves. Whatever they were doing, they were getting the best output. If you have positive thinking for becoming successful, no one would be able to propel you in any other (wrong) direction, as you are committed towards movement only towards your goal.

Doing something because you like the work and doing something with a positive attitude are two different concepts altogether. The former is directly proportional to your interest and as soon as you lose interest, you lose the concentration in work. In latter case, attitude forces you not to give up, despite negative intermediate results till you achieve your target.

Make the thing to happen

People, who had earned a name in this world either during their life-time or after their death were those who made the things happen in the way they wanted to make them happen. They did not wait to take the time to decide a course of action but they did it in the way they wanted. Individuals, who possess such instincts, shape the world according to their own thinking. Obstacles are there but they utilize such obstacles to propel their actions towards the coveted goals instead of surrendering to those obstacles.

You should be able to recall the story of the thirsty crow. Two classes of thinking are associated with it. One group would strongly believe that the crow should not have done so much labour for getting the water out of the pitcher. Rather, he should have searched an alternative source of water. The second group will be of the opinion, "If you don't take a stand on anything, then everything will slip from your hands". Neither of the two genres of thought is right or wrong. But one thing is very clear that the class of thinking reflects your attitude. In the first style you are a deserter. You can't be relied on and seeing a strong opposition, you will immediately change your views and way of action. In the second style, you will search for alternatives to solve any difficult situation to suit you.

If you don't take a stand on anything, then everything will slip from your hands.

Basically, everyone has the same quantity of blood, number of (or almost similar) bones, neurons and other vital specifications. The difference lies in attitude. Attitude is directly related to your "Self Concept" which is your worth. You can't do anything more than your worth which gets shaped through your 'Self'. The physical shape of a body is in no way any indication of strong or weak attitude. A strong and healthy person may have a weak attitude whereas a very lean and thin person might possess strong attitude. The formation of attitude is the combined result of your worth and your evaluation about yourself.

You must have witnessed an elephant tied with a rope. It is amazing that the biggest animal on this earth which has enormous strength to uproot the biggest banyan tree (to which it is tied) stands there as if he had no strength. It happens because just after its birth, its master ties it like this. This typing, with chain lowers the little elephants attitude that it has been tied strongly and can't get out of it without the help of his master. This very concept overpowers its own strength.

Most of us are like that elephant and never try to break the worldly ties to do something according to our worth. That is because since our childhood, we are being taught that "big work is meant for big people." On the contrary, it is a fact that "big work has always been done by "small individuals". However, the time we realize this fact, it is already too late. Strange enough, we never learn a lesson; nor we teach the same to our posterity, as we are fearful of ourselves and make them helpless individuals.

Those, who dare to break the trend, get something better for them and society. In the beginning one needs more energy to break the trend but as one proceeds, the self-generated worth is more than enough to propel one further to achieve what one something.

You may feel–if it was so easy to succeed or achieve goals, why couldn't everyone be a successful individual in his area of operation. Everyone starts direction by breaking the weak bonds that had held him for long. He proceeds further with a firm belief of achieving something better but immediately, he gets surrounded by some circumstances which create a fear within him that he will be a looser, so, he terried even as he tries to achieve what he wanted to. Finally he retreats or even stops is pursuit. Most of us feel that if someone else in society is unable to achieve the goal which he has been eyeing, he may not be able to achieve the same either, as it may require something special which he may or may not be possessing. People are like tied elephants with a thin rope. They see one another and get a feeling that if the strongest one can't break the rope, it also can't do so. This thinking goes on from generation to generation. The same tenet applies to us too.

We take everything on its face value and hardly bother to go into the detail to find the exact position. On the day, we make ourselves ready to face any challenge, we shall proceed on our journey towards our goal. It is also sure that it will not be a smooth sail for anyone. Had this been so easy, everyone would have been in a position to achieve the same. Even if the journey of success is tough, so many people achieve what they wanted, they change their attitude, for (from weak to strong) and that makes all the difference.

Once you achieve something in the direction of your thoughts your attitude gets strengthened and you get propelled further with some extra energy. Thus, you go on achieving what you exactly wanted. People will always be there to put a stiff resistance through their unwanted advice or actions but you have to ignore the same politely, without hurting the sentiments of such individuals. Otherwise, they may create more unwanted problems and you have to kill your precious time in solving the same.

You need not indulge yourself in fighting or teaching lessons to others, else the enemy would come to know your true worth. It is the fight of worth only and in no way, people would be able to evaluate your actual worth. As your worth directly shapes your attitude, you should be careful about such situations let people get a vague idea about yourself to keep on guessing your true worth.

> **Don't indulge yourself in fighting or teaching lessons to others, else the enemy would come to know your true worth.**

Failure is natural

Failure attracts attention more than success does. Very few people would be interested to know the steps which you had taken to be successful but most people would be interested in knowing the steps which had led you to failure.

No one wants to learn from the failures of others one feels that circumstances which had led to the failure of someone, may not give the same result to one. Note that circumstances are non-living and their behavioural pattern is fixed for everyone. People are generally comfortable while experiencing failure themselves. The individuals who postmortem their failure, not for being critical of anyone but to learn a lesson, are successful at a later stage. Thus, they would avoid those stages which lead them to failure. When you fail in your endeavour, you immediately realize that "if you lose everything, still the 'future' is in your hands."

If you lose everything, still the 'future' is in your hands.

People like us forget to realize that there is not a fixed path to a particular destination. Till you don't reach to your destination, don't infer that the destination is not there but immediately search for an alternate path.The possibility is that it may lead you to your destination, thus making you comfortable.

Success and failure are same, as both are 'identities'. The thing which you take as 'success' may not be 'success' to someone else. The situation which you are taking as a 'failure' may be "success" to someone else. The best property of 'identities' is that their meaning changes with person, place and time. The success which is making you happy now may not keep you happy for a longer period. That is because its effect will cease over a period of time and you need some bigger event of success than the previous one to be happy. It goes on but the end never comes. That is why it has been said that success is not destination but a journey. A journey keeps you vibrant whereas a destination makes you stationary.

It is your own thinking which makes you happy or unhappy about success or failure; it is directly proportional to your attitude and worth. If you have not evaluated your worth, a small success will give you more happiness, as your attitude has been shaped accordingly, so you get relaxed and have a feeling that you have achieved what you wanted to achieve.

The words 'success' and 'failure' are very personalized. These personalized words cannot be subjected to scientific analysis and scrutiny. You must define your success to measure your progress. It is a must, otherwise you would fall into a vicious circle of confusion and very little progress would give you happiness and a little failure would bring you to the floor, in a state of desperation and failure. Both are extreme situations which you must avoid. This is possible only if you define your own concepts of success and failure.

An old man was disturbed due to his loneliness. The only son and his wife were working and they hardly had time for the old man. The only grand daughter was always busy in her studies. She did not get some time to talk even to her parents, leave alone her grandfather. Being disturbed with his pathetic loneliness he went to a sea shore and started walking on the sand.

Suddenly he heard a voice, "Catch and kiss me." He ignored the voice but the voice kept on chasing him. He looked on the ground and saw a frog. He picked up from the ground and the frog said, "Kiss me". Suddenly, he remembered old story which reminded him of the talking frog that turned into a gorgeous lady after being kissed by a prince.

The old man put the talking frog inside his pocket. The frog was shouting again and again and requesting to be kissed. The old man took him out from his pocket and said, "Look, at this age, I am least interested to get company of a gorgeous lady. However, I certainly need the company of a 'talking frog' stating this, he slipped the frog in his pocket yet again.

The thing and situation which makes you happy once may not be able to elicit the same response over a period. Once you achieve something, you ignore its significance and try to get something more than that. It is essential to have such a feeling because you have to keep on moving. Failure is a stationary action where as, success is a non-stationery action, as it forces you to do better and still better all the time.

Mistakes are a boon

You always need someone to punish you and make you understand your actual position. The mistakes committed in life help you achieve the same. Once you commit any mistake, you suffer loss and learn a lesson. You also vouch not to commit s uch mistakes in the future. Mistakes are your teachers. They help you become careful in attaining something in life either for yourself or for the organization you work for.

If you need new ideas, you have to create a fear-free environment around you so that people can give suggestions and speak up. All suggestions can't be of any help to you but they may provoke your thinking in the required direction. No idea and no book, how worst it may be, can be totally rubbish. Above all, every individual has some price and you don't know which idea turns out to be worth a million Dollars for you.

A individual, who is afraid of committing mistakes, can't do anything, as he would be afraid of mistakes. Such individual forget the basic theory that people in this world like the individual who has some worth and are not idle. If you don't do anything, it means you would not be noticed. If you are not noticed, you are not alive. Scientifically you may be alive but in reality you are not an entity at all.

You must have heard people commenting that they avoid committing any mistake. There is nothing wrong in it but if you will carefully observe, you would find that they are the people who always find faults in others. In any organization, there would be a group that would neither do anything nor allow someone to do a little extra. It would do so by creating a fear of failure amongst them so that they should avoid committing mistakes. The individuals, who come out of their influence are able to do something and get recognition. The people, who make a mark in life, are those who think of something new and come forward to put their abilities to test.

The people, who do not do anything, never commit mistakes.

You can control the fear perceived by you but it may be very difficult to come out of the fear created for you by others. Sometimes, the latter goes too deep to be removed and no one else would be of any help to you, except yourself. You must be ready to face the situation with a firm belief that heaven is not going to fall if you commit a mistake. Further you must foresee the worst which can happen by committing a mistake. You would find a sudden change in your thinking with such notions. Such notions would be of great help in shaping your destiny.

While working on a school project in the remotest corner of Rajasthan, I had become very friendly with that school owner; it was a known business house of India. One day, I received mail in my mail box with the subject 'Help' from the owner. It had come as it was a surprise to me. I immediately opened the mail and came to know that it was a forwarded mail of one of his IITian friends who ran a management institute. This friend, as I came to know later on, had not taken the recognition of an affiliating body of such institutes as they demanded something which was not as per his ethos. Later, on this very ground, a parent had filed an FIR of fraud and cheating against that institute.

I was told that the institute was always right and personal grudges were there against all these things. The man wrote to my gentleman's client to help him get out of the situation. I requested a police officer, a friend of mine, to help me and to my utter surprise, he was helpful. In the beginning, I thought that in case I was unable to handle the situation, I might spoil my reputation. But as I was not fearful of my mistakes in handling the case, so I became successful.

Life would give you many chances. You should all of them but you would be able to make use of some of them. It can happen only when you are not fearful of your mistakes, otherwise you would be too conscious about your actions. The chances are that you would lose the game. Doing something with firm belief in yourself, without fear of consequences makes all the difference. Whether you are on the lower ladder of management or on the top level, the situation in both cases is almost similar. In any position, you must feel yourself better placed than others to take the right decision under all conditions, favourable or unfavourable.

Mistakes are the building blocks of your success story. No one in this world has achieved anything without committing mistakes during his journey of success. The only thing is that once you are successful in your project, you and the people around you forget the mistakes committed by you. In case the project is unsuccessful, you remember only the committed mistakes and not the right steps which you had undertook during the journey. It happens with everyone. There are very few daredevils who immediately take other routes after coming to know their mistakes and don't spend a lot of time in doing the postmortem of their committed mistakes. They feel that 'to err is human' and everyone faces the same consequences.

It is the state of mind which makes all the difference. If you feel that you are defeated due to some of your mistakes, you are. But contrary to that, if you feel that there is always an alternative left after committing any mistake, you have won half the battle. Prepare yourself for facing the worst even when things are moving as per your calculation. This policy would as it will help you recover immediately after a shock.

Feel comfortable wherever you are

We are living in a society in which from the childhood, we are taught to have a win-win attitude and our personality gets shaped accordingly. We imbibe a habit to compromise and feel that we are doing a great service to society. The killer instinct, is absent in most of us. We are firm believers of equality. We forget the basic rule of nature that we can't be equal and excellent at one point of time. In order to be excellent, we have to be unequal.

I have interacted with teachers during my training programmes. I used to ask them why they did not have a smiling facial expression? I told them that it helped their students learn better. The simple answer I used to get was that it was the demand of the profession. On further enquiry, I used to learn that they never saw their department head that was happy with them. They thought. That there angry face might be helpful in getting better results in the classroom. The gloomy look of the teacher forces students to become withdrawn, even absent from the class.

Although the situations in the classrooms have changed up to some extent due to the induction of fresh blood in the system new teachers need a lot of time to prove that they have been accepted by their students. In the way the student's attitude has changed, the teachers attitude has not changed. There are several reasons behind it. Previously, teacher used to be the only source of inspiration but students are the product of one hundred and eighty channels and the Net. When any information set is obtained by clicking the mouse, these the teachers redundant. They hate all these modern gadgets since they have challenged their identity in classrooms.

They feel themselves too old to learn to work with these modern gadgets. They also hate and making new gadgets to improve their performance. They can't believe that all these gadgets can never replace a teacher in the classroom. These are all cosmetics which can bring brightness to a face if used properly. You may believe it or not but the teaching community has always felt itself insecure.

> **Your victory is not a guarantee of victory but you must have the wish to win at all times.**

During my training sessions with teachers, I try to emphasize that they would always win in life, is not a guarantee but you must have the wish to win at all times.

When you are not able to take an independent decision, you become a victim of "burn out" as you get exhausted by repeating the same exercise again and again. An independent thinker gets energy for thinking ahead.

You should not feel yourself less rewarded than others, irrespective of the profession you have chosen to work in. Keep your self-respect high in every situation to deliver the best in your area of operation. Rest assured, brilliants workers or performers are still required in bulk in any field. Try to update yourself wherever you are and do your best. This 'best' shall give you satisfaction of working in an environment which may be a dream for others. You don't know when you will get the reward of your hard and meticulous labour. Only thinking is not sufficient; you must also work in your field to make yourself the best. Decide now and start working forgetting the place of work or other not-so-good conditions.

Always have the wish to win

You must have noticed individuals around you who always blame circumstances or some other individuals for their failure. They are unable to realize the basic fact of life that a successful individual has no time to pull anyone down. If you fall or fail, it is purely due to your thinking and working and the role of others is almost negligible.

All of us are eyeing success. Some of us go on exploring the alternate path when they are unsuccessful after following a particular path. Some people stop trying after a single defeat and devote the time to find 'scape goat' for our failures. This leads to frustration and makes us incompetent for ever. We fail to realize that it is the size of one's will which determines success.

It is the size of one's will which determines success.

The wish to win is a state of mind and is a learnable behaviour. It has to be practiced. It goes so deep that this behaviour gets mingled with our personality. Such individuals can be recognized in a crowd due to their behavioural features. Time and again, they want satisfaction through quality and set their goals by evaluating all pros and cons. They also keep scope for contingencies coming in their way.

If you have a wish to win, you must be aloof of all bouquets and brick bats. These two factors adversely affect the process, thus we are discussing now. Praise raises your self-esteem forcing you to take uncalculated risk for which neither you are physically nor mentally prepared. The same is the case with criticism. It lowers your self-esteem , so you are unable to think anything good for your improvement. It has been psychologically proved through different studies that individuals having balanced self-concept are able to achieve their goal easily and in the shortest span of time.

Sometimes, conditions may force you to take a small nap during your journey of success to recharge yourself and evaluate your circumstances. These small breaks are given by nature but we may confused it with our failure and stop our journey in the middle. It happens, as nature also wants to judge our capabilities so that success might not go to wrong hands. Once we know the basic actions of 'nature' we leave our tasks midway but we always become go getter.

Most of us start our journey of success with a firm belief to win but it does not happen to most of us. The only reason of this setback is that we are not able to sustain the jerks of success. These jerks are in the form of severe setbacks. Sometimes, we are very near success but we are unable to view the same and desert the goal, thinking that it is too difficult to get. While breaking a big boulder, we go on hitting the boulder till we break it into pieces. If we do not put the last stroke, the desired result can't be achieved. Not only this, we can't say that the first and the second stroke was of no use or was not as effective as the last one. Making the first stroke was as essential as the last stroke. The same is the case for achieving success in any other field of life. Every step taken towards the goal has its own value and each step is the precursor of the next step.

As the definition of the success differs with person to person; so does its method. For some, success means getting the desired that may be as small as a low priced car. For other, it may be getting a white-collar job. For some others, it is donating money every year as fees of ten poor students to a public school. As the definition of success differs from one individual to another, so does the way of achieving success. But one thing is common to all and that is the gravity of achieving the success and the processes. With different process everyone is eyeing a product which gives almost same soothing feeling to all.

Your first work is to prepare yourself for the journey of success, as the preparation takes a lot of time. It takes time, as you have to evaluate yourself and your goal and then synchronize the steps in the right direction. One basic factor you have to keep in mind is that success is an inner state of mind and it takes shape due to self-motivation so it may require more self-energy than any external force. The only requirement is to remove your thinking that you can be a failure. Have a firm believe in your capacity and competencies to feel that you have all the required qualities to be a successful individual. Your belief in yourself would be acting as an external force to move you towards your goal. The factors, which bring success, are the same for every individual who starts with a firm belief to get success. Those, who achieve success, are people who never allow their energy level to come down at any point of time of their journey. They get vitalized by getting small doses of success on the way, for they feel that success is a journey and this journey shall never end.

You can do it

You must have heard so many times from your elders and teachers that most great wars were won as the winner had a will to win and in most cases, the opponent was much stronger than the winner. The will decides your destiny and it shall get shaped due to persistent thinking in the direction. The top mountain climbers, would admit that there will was the best decisive factor in the course of reaching the top.

> **The difference between a successful person and others is not the lack of strength or knowledge but lack of will.**

The will of getting anything special is generated when you miss something in your life. In order to fill the gap you think in different directions and try to get help from each corner so that you could get the same. The process goes on indefinitely, till you are able to get a concrete shape of your thinking. Once it is imprinted in your mind, it forces you to move in the desired direction time and again.

There was a famous wrestler who used to defeat any of his team members and sometimes, even his coach during the daily practice session. But he used to be nervous whenever he was in the middle of a competition. His teacher was worried and unable to find what to do about his nervousness. One day, he told everything to his friend who was a spiritual teacher. As per his advice, the wrestler was sent to his worship place in the evening. The spiritual teacher asked his name and he answered "Strom." The teacher appreciated his name and told him how he liked to be thunder in reality, just like his name.

The wrestler thought for while and unconsciously, he was reminded of big a storm which creates havoc on the earth. Suddenly, he opened his eyes and felt a miraculous change in himself. After that, he was never defeated in any competition. It was his will to succeed that had removed his hesitation.

You may have all the ingredients that may be necessary to be successful but until you have the will, all these ingredients are of no use. The will of doing a thing is the most important ingredient required for getting that thing done. If one has no will, one can't make the thing happen; rather he will wait for the thing to happen.

There is no dearth of strongest and wisest individuals on this earth and you may have noticed a number of them around you but they are not sure of what they want in their life. They are satisfied by what they get and take it as their destiny. For the time being they may appear to be successful individuals but in reality, they are not. One can't be successful without having a will to be successful, irrespective of all other qualities which one possesses. That is because the other qualities are as important as the will.

Most of us are not aware of the role of will in our life. We start any piece of work that if someone else is doing that we would also be able to do it. There is nothing wrong in this thinking except we forget to compare the will which is the deciding factor for making someone successful and someone failure. Keeping your will in a clicking position is also a very difficult task, as it gets shaken as and when we get shock of failure in life. That time is of immense importance to a person who is moving towards a goal. It happens as we never want a set back in our life and get frustrated with a setback irrespective of our age and experience. You might have seen an entrepreneur who starts a venture and desert the same in the middle with one hundred excuses, without blaming themselves. It is due to their shattered will.

If you have the will, do whatever you like and be sure that you shall be successful, irrespective of the jerks you would be encountering on your way. The factor, which is responsible for making you successful is your will and all other factors are of supplementary nature only. Your will boosts your self-confidence and becomes instrumental in achieving everything that you want.

Unlock your potential

In order to get the desired result according to your will, you are required to unlock your potential. You are not less than anyone, you have all the qualities and capabilities required to be successful. Possibilities are there that you may not have evaluated your potentials. Alternatively, you may not have tapped your potential. Potential is the inborn quality which every individual possess since birth. You have to do continuous effort to unlock your potential. An individual need more intelligent or have more strength than others to unlock his potential.

Continuous efforts – not strength or intelligence – are the key so unlocking your potential.

Efforts are required to do any work and continuous effort is the key to success. Most of us start any piece of work with all commitments but desert the same in the middle. It happens as very few of us are devoted towards our goal and desert the same as soon as some problems strike us. It gives us a feeling that we have decided a wrong destination and try to locate some other easy and different goals. We forget that any goal, if chosen properly, with due consideration of our own worth after proper evaluation, has almost similar difficulty level. It is only our thinking which makes all the difference.

Continuous effort is the key to success. The effort should be planned in such a way that at any point of time, the strike rate should not be less than the previous one. It is same as constructing a house from scratch.

Man, by his nature, does not have the habit of making continuous efforts in spite of the fact that it is a learnable behaviour. Being a learnable behaviour through a constant practice, it is not difficult to learn it. Once this characteristic is acquired by an individual, he will never fail in his efforts. The only thing is that this habit has to be inculcated from early childhood, as a child can learn anything easily. With his growth this behaviour gets embedded in his mind in due course of time. It is not as easy as a child can't concentrate on anything for a longer span of time. Once the distracters, which do not allow to maintain his concentration, are removed, the chances are there to get positive results.

Distracters are always there in everyone's life and can't be avoided. In order to get the final result one has to learn to control these distracters. These distracters are in the form of easy achievement and false impression of achievement. A person, who is strong in his thinking, can control these distracters. Make yourself mentally strong to overcome the distractors.

Be Firm

A king of Persia was fond of his Prime Minister due to his logical and critical thinking and the advice given to the king in regarding the kingdom's operations. The king became so dependent that he did not think of continuing as the king without his Prime Minister, once, the king became seriously annoyed with his PM. He tried to control his anger but all in vein. In this angry state of mind, he ordered his men to hang the PM.

The order was passed to the PM next day when he was busy celebrating the birthday of his dear daughter. As the message spread, everyone become frustrated and the celebration was stopped.

Upon enquiry the PM came to know that all the celebration had been stopped. He ordered everything to be resumed immediately and asked the messenger to convey the king that he would report at the hanging ground after finishing the celebration of the birthday of his daughter.

The king listened to this news of celebration. He thought for a while. Then he cancelled the order to hang the PM. He told those who were around him a person is not fearful of his death, nothing can distract him from doing the right act.

Most of us are firm and have a belief that nothing can distract us from doing right thing. However, but very few of us stand firm after a setback. A small setback may not distract us but when it is the question of survival only a few of us stick to our decision and those who stick to get the fruit of success. Once you believe that everything is destined, there is no question of surrendering in front of difficulties and if you don't believe in destiny and believe only in hard work, then nothing would be able to distract you. It is only your belief which makes you a winner or a looser, all other facts are transitory and have a very short life span.

Always be firm with your action so that people may have faith in you. This would also give boost to your self-esteem and propel you towards your goal. The king in the story tried to shake the belief of his minister in himself but he was not successful, as the minister was firm with his decision. He knew that he is not in the wrong foot.

Footprints on the sands of time are not made by just sitting down.

•

About the Authors

Mrs. Indu Pandey

Mrs. Indu Pandey was born in 1965. She is a social worker by profession. She put forth the idea of setting up the Pandey Education Trust. She finally fulfilled her dream of starting this trust in 1995, in the memory of her Late father-in-law, Shri S.N. Pandey. Mrs Indu Pandey has contributed greatly towards the operations of success of the trust which is an institution in itself now. She is an HR expert. She gives support to the academic experts in the field of education.

Dr. A.K. Pandey

Dr. A.K. Pandey was born in 1956. He is the CEO of the Pandey Education Trust. He is a renowned motivator and trainer of teachers. He has trained more than 2000 teachers till date. More than 35 of his research papers have been published in journals of repute, including *Indian Education Review* and *NHRD*. He has been awarded by the PTA and Jetty Foundation. He is also a visiting faculty at the International School of Management, Jaipur. He has achieved many landmarks in the field of education management. You may reach the authors at edutrust@rediffmail.com

By the same authors

- **What if you die tomorrow?**
- **Crack the Shell That Covers You**
- **Zid Karo Safalta Pao**